B FELLINI

Burke, Frank.

Federico Fellini

Twayne's Filmmakers Series

Warren French
EDITOR

Federico Fellini:
Variety Lights to *La Dolce Vita*

The frontispiece shows Fellini preparing to shoot a scene for La Dolce Vita. *Courtesy: Cinemabilia*

Federico Fellini:
Variety Lights to *La Dolce Vita*

FRANK BURKE

University of Manitoba

BOSTON

Twayne Publishers

1984

Federico Fellini:
Variety Lights to *La Dolce Vita*

is first published in 1984 by Twayne Publishers
A Division of G. K. Hall & Company

Copyright © 1984 by G. K. Hall & Company
All Rights Reserved

Book Production by Marne B. Sultz

Printed on permanent/durable acid-free paper and
bound in the United States of America

First Printing, October 1984

Library of Congress Cataloging in Publication Data

Burke, Frank.
Federico Fellini : Variety Lights to La Dolce Vita.

(Twayne's filmmakers series)
Bibliography: p. 133
Includes index.
1. Fellini, Federico. I. Title. II. Series.
PN1998.A3F333   1984   791.43′0233′0924   84-9050
ISBN 0-8057-9300-3

Contents

About the Author   vi

Editor's Foreword   vii

Preface   xi

Acknowledgments   xv

Chronology   xvii

1. Fellini, Italian Neorealism, and the Contours of Vision   1

2. *Variety Lights*   7

3. *The White Sheik*   13

4. *I Vitelloni*   21

5. "A Matrimonial Agency"   31

6. *La Strada*   37

7. *Il Bidone*   55

8. *The Nights of Cabiria*   69

9. *La Dolce Vita*   85

10. Summing Up: Fellini's Development Through *La Dolce Vita*   101

11. Intermezzo: "The Temptations of Dr. Antonio"   115

Notes and References   127

Selected Bibliography   133

Filmography (1950–62)   138

Index   142

About the Author

Frank Burke is a New Yorker by birth, a Winnipegger by current fate, and a Roman by projection. He fell under the spell of Fellini and film at the University of Florida, assisted by the light of W. R. Robinson's imagination. He has taught film and American literature at the University of Kentucky; he currently teaches film theory and criticism at the University of Manitoba. He has published essays on Wertmuller, Antonioni, Fellini, Peckinpah, and film theory.

Editor's Foreword

At the conclusion of "David Lean: A Self-Portrait," the director, one of the great traditionalists, who explains through this film his life's work, comments that he does not believe the movies have yet produced artists who are capable of "making great statements about life." I disagree. In the foreword to Michael Anderegg's recent book about David Lean for this generally auteurist-oriented series, I make some summary statements, embroidering upon the pioneer theorizings of François Truffaut and Andrew Sarris, about the difference between auteurs and *metteurs-en-scène*, using Federico Fellini and Lean, respectively, as examples of two breeds of filmmakers indispensable to what Abel Gance called the "Seventh Art."

Contemplating Federico Fellini, I would agree not with David Lean, but with Dino De Laurentiis, producer of some of Fellini's first masterpieces. Although this canny entrepreneur is sometimes minimized as being only interested in what he can make *from* the movies, he has been astute enough to acknowledge that Ingmar Bergman and Federico Fellini stand apart from their contemporaries in what they can make *of* the cinema. Both do have something—and I think something significant—to say about the great problems of our own century and all human experience. I think that *The Seventh Seal* and *Fellini-Satyricon, Juliet of the Spirits* and *Fanny and Alexander* deserve their places among the great creations of the human imagination and the human spirit.

When we planned this series of books nearly a decade ago, I hankered to provide the tribute to Fellini myself. I had a particular hobbyhorse I wanted to ride. I wanted to establish Fellini, starting from what I consider the remarkable parallels between *La Dolce Vita* and James Joyce's short-story cycle *Dubliners*, as the artist who belatedly brought to film the modernist sensibility as Joyce had at the beginning of this century brought it to fiction. I had first discovered Fellini during that marvelous summer of 1961 when *La Dolce Vita* revolutionized (and revelationized) our expectations of film during its premiere American showing at New York's Henry Miller's theater. There was enormous excitement among filmophiles then about Fellini; but as new works appeared and old ones were rediscovered, factions not surprisingly developed. I became outraged, however, at those critics who began to argue, as Frank Burke points out, that Fellini's later films were "undisciplined, self-indulgent, irrational, unintelligible." I wanted to set the record straight.

I could not, however, create the time and resources to carry out this self-imposed task, even if, as I considered essential, I had mastered Italian. Perhaps this is just as well; for my failures in the quest are themselves evidence of an imaginative inadequacy for the project. Rather I have had the good fortune to sponsor a book that has enabled me—as I think it will others—to discover more about Fellini than I had perceived myself.

As soon as I came to my senses about my responsibilities to this series, I began searching for a surrogate to give Fellini what had to be his respected place in it. I have not always agreed with contributors to this series about the evaluation of their subjects, and I have tried to maintain as open-minded a forum as possible within the general framework of an auteurist-oriented approach. But there could be no compromise with Fellini. I could not endorse a study that did not adequately appreciate his unique vision.

I looked at proposals and read articles about Fellini without enthusiasm. Then Frank Burke wrote to me about his developing theories. When I responded by explaining bluntly my particular concern for this project that would make me more than usually demanding, he agreed to undertake it anyway. After several meetings with him, I felt confident that I had made the right choice.

That was some time ago. If, as Frank argues and I agree, "the struggle for self-realization . . . is, above all else, the 'Fellini story'" (see the end of chapter 2), so this same struggle for self-realization—a slow and painful matter—must lie behind an adequate criticism of Fellini. This book has thus been longer in the making than either of us anticipated. Even now, the work is but half realized, for in the early planning of the series, it had been agreed there must be two volumes about Fellini in order to provide adequate analysis of such puzzling and controversial creations. I had originally planned to divide the books between 8½ and *Juliet of the Spirits*, since Fellini's move from black and white to color for his major features seemed to me to mark also a switch from works characterized by an artist's gray uncertainty about the confidence he could feel in his own vision unless it were relentlessly despairing about human possibilities, to more than naturally colorful works embodying the artist's confidence in his vision to transcend the world's squalor and illuminate the way people *could* change whether they *would* or not.

Frank was originally willing to go along with this plan; but his much longer and deeper involvement than mine with the films led him to put the emphasis upon a great change between *La Dolce Vita* and 8½ that involved far more aspects of Fellini's work than the simplistic one I had originally proposed. He showed me that not just a change in vision, but experimentation with narrative techniques and aesthetic principles to communicate the vision must be encompassed by an adequate criticism.

To him I leave the presentation of the evidence supporting his position that Fellini seeks to create not traditional works, but "vehicles for the examination of various imaginative possibilities."

It remains only to be said that there is more to come. Even though *Fellini I* will be one of the last regularly scheduled offerings in this series, Frank is at work on *Fellini II*. Thus Fellini has succeeded again in transcending a format that threatened to limit him as we look forward to a consideration of his achievement from 8½ to. . . .

W. F.

Preface

I have tried to approach Fellini in a manner that is consistent and applicable in equal measure to all his films—in short, true to his art as a whole. I view his films as narrative processes vitally concerned with the quality of human experience. I try to demonstrate how these processes cohere, and I try to determine what Fellini has to say about the struggle and responsibility of being human. Also, I try to establish that Fellini's early career is, in itself, a coherent "narrative" of imaginative growth.

In emphasizing values such as experience, imagination, and formal coherence, I part company with contemporary critical theorists such as the deconstructionists who deny the individual as a unified subject of experience and deny the text as a unified structure. Unlike these theorists, I still believe in an aesthetic impulse—a quest for experienced, embodied, communicable wholeness—which can be realized in extraordinary ways through narrative art. I trust the instincts of an artist such as William Carlos Williams who, in discussing his enormously complex *Paterson*, emphasizes formalist notions: "[since completing *Paterson, Four*] I had to take Paterson into a new dimension. . . . Yet I wanted to keep it *whole*, as it is to me. As I mulled the thing over in my mind the *composition* began to assume a new *form* which you see in the present poem keeping, I fondly hope, *a unity directly continuous with* the Paterson of *Pat. 1* to *4*."[1] Williams's remarks are especially interesting since *Paterson* has become one of the beloved texts of those American critics who prize *differance* and indeterminacy over formal coherence. John Dewey has emphasized the vital importance of the aesthetic impulse in terms thoroughly consistent with the spirit of Fellini's vision:

The sense of an extensive and underlying whole is the context of every experience and it is the essence of sanity. . . . A work of art elicits and accentuates this quality of being whole and of belonging to the larger, all-inclusive, whole which is the universe in which we live. . . . Where egotism is not made the measure of reality and value, we are citizens of this vast world beyond ourselves, and any intense realization of its presence with and in us brings a peculiarly satisfying sense of unity in itself and with ourselves.[2]

If current approaches to film comprised a spectrum ranging from the cool blues of objective analysis to the warm reds of subjective response, mine would clearly fall closer to the blues. I tend to avoid impressionistic discussion of emotional impact. I find that people's responses to film are highly personal, often idiosyncratic, and seldom fully shared. (I even know someone who finds the characters in *La Strada* quite stupid and not worth his bother!)

At the same time, I try to avoid the coldness, the forbidding objectivity, of pure formalism, which belabors cinematic technique just for the sake of technique. I address the cinematic dimension of Fellini's work only as it becomes an integral part of the kinds of stories he is telling. Because his earliest films are more dramatic than cinematic, technique does not begin to become a crucial factor until *The Nights of Cabiria* (1956). By "The Temptations of Dr. Antonio" (1962), both technique and film aesthetics become quite crucial and are treated accordingly. (To give formalism its due, I indicate in chapters 10–11 that, to my mind, Fellini acquires his greatest significance as an artist when he begins to "discover" his medium in films such as "Dr. Antonio" and *8½*.) Although my method is more objective than subjective, my concern with human value and experience is meant to provide a basis for determining why Fellini's films have resonance and relevance for others—why they evoke profound emotional responses.

In terms of providing translations of Italian dialogue, I have relied on existing sources—subtitles and English screenplays—whenever possible. My intent was to use sources with which the English reader is already familiar—and which have already contributed to the reader's experience of the films. In some instances, for the sake of accuracy, I have had to provide my own translations. *La Dolce Vita* proved particularly problematic because of numerous discrepancies among the actual dialogue, the subtitles, and the English screenplay. I found myself relying variously on subtitles, the screenplay, and my own translations in order to provide the most helpful renderings from the Italian.

One seldom surrenders a manuscript for publication without regret. It became clearer with each film I discussed—and as Fellini's imagination gathered momentum—that no critical approach could approximate in scope the richness of Fellini's vision. So much had to be eliminated in the interests of preserving some semblance of flow. As a result, each discussion provides a mere skeleton, not only of Fellini's work, but of the total information that can be derived from a narrative analysis of his films.

My greatest regret is that my critical method does not reflect more fully the spirit of Fellini's vision. Despite its commitment to the nature of experience in Fellini's films, the method remains *about* experience without becoming truly experiential. Because this first volume focuses on moral implications, which are often rather grim in the early films, I am not able to give full expression to Fellini's marvelous humor. Finally, despite my desire to see Fellini as concretely as possible, I inevitably (dealing as I must in language and concept) "intellectualize" his work. Fellini would be the first to object!

Nonetheless, I hope the following can serve as a signpost (to borrow a notion from Dewey), guiding the reader more precisely to certain important aspects of Fellini's art and making that art accessible in new and rewarding ways. The point of it all is *not* to offer some definitive interpretation of Fellini nor to effect some sort of critical consensus. It is to tempt the reader back to Fellini's movies, where the aesthetic experience itself can—as it must—be the final arbiter of value.

FRANK BURKE

University of Manitoba

Acknowledgments

My thanks are due first of all to those who have made Fellini's movies available to me: Myron Bresnick (Audio Brandon), Saul Turell (Janus Films), and Doug Brooker (formerly with IFD). I have received assistance far beyond the call of duty from media resource specialists: Paul Owen (University of Kentucky) and Nancy Lane and Irene Thain (University of Manitoba). I have also been generously funded by the University of Manitoba and the Social Sciences and Humanities Research Council of Canada.

I am most grateful to the Canadian Academic Centre in Italy for providing facilities and assistance while I was completing final revisions of my manuscript.

Some of the material in this volume has appeared (usually in far different contexts) in *Italica, Literature/Film Quarterly, Film Criticism,* the *Canadian Journal of Political and Social Theory, North Dakota Quarterly, Film Studies: Proceedings of the Sixth Annual Purdue University Conference on Film,* and *Proceedings of the Fifth Annual Purdue University Conference on Film.* I thank these publications for allowing the material to appear again here.

I thank Bill Robinson, who showed me that I had eyes but saw not—then did all he could to help remedy the situation. He made the movies move (for) me. I thank Warren French for his faith, patience, moral support, friendship, and editorial advice—in short, for making the book happen. Then there are Walt Foreman, Steve Snyder, and Armando Prats, who have aided me immeasurably in my appreciation of Fellini. Dick Sugg, Ed Stanton, and Bob O'Kell have been colleagues for all seasons; George Toles has been a most helpful reader of my works-in-progress; Gene Walz and Daniel Phelan have provided invaluable bibliographical updating on Fellini; Ben Lawton and Peter Bondanella have provided crucial professional support and encouragement. I thank Walt (again) for his scrupulous editorial work on the manuscript, Sandi Lawrie for her equally scrupulous secretarial assistance.

Most of all, there are family debts: to my parents, to the Clarks, and to Val, Tyler, and Wylie, who have provided the emotional funding that has made my work on Fellini possible.

Chronology

1920	Federico Fellini born on 20 January in Rimini, a small town on the Adriatic Sea, son of provincial bourgeoisie parents.
ca. 1928	Runs away from school (or so he has claimed in certain interviews) and spends brief period with the circus.
1938	Goes to Florence. Does comic-strips for Nerbini.
1939–1940	Moves to Rome. Works as reporter for three weeks on *Il popolo*. Joins editorial staff of *Marc' Aurelio*. Begins writing sketches for radio and gags for the movies.
1941–1943	Comedian and actor Aldo Fabrizi helps him get scriptwriting jobs in movies. Marries Giulietta Masina. Saved from the draft when an air raid destroys his medical records.
1944	Giulietta gives birth to a son who lives only three weeks. After Rome is liberated, Fellini and friends open several "Funny Face Shops" to draw characters for Allied soldiers.
1945	Meets director Roberto Rossellini and becomes involved in the script for *Roma, Città Aperta (Rome, Open City)*.
1946	Works as screenwriter and assistant director on *Paisà (Paisan)*.
1947	Writes and acts in *Il Miracolo (The Miracle*, director Rossellini). Works with director Alberto Lattuada on *Il Delitto di Giovanni Episcopo*.
1948	Works with Lattuada on *Senza Pietà* and *Il Mulino del Po;* with Pietro Germi on *In Nome della Legge*.
1949	Works as scriptwriter and assistant director with Rossellini on *Francesco, Giullare di Dio*.
1950	Co-directs *Luci del Varietà (Variety Lights)* with Lattuada; works with Germi on *Il Cammino della Speranza*.
1951	Works with Germi on *La Città si Difende*.

1952   Debuts as sole director with *Lo Sciecco Bianco (The White Sheik)*. Works with Germi on *Il Brigante di Tacca del Lupo*.

1953   *I Vitelloni* wins Silver Lion Award at Venice Film Festival; first Fellini film to receive international distribution. "Un'agenzia matrimoniale" ("A Matrimonial Agency") appears as part of a film anthology entitled *Amore in Città (Love in the City)*, produced by Cesare Zavattini.

1954   *La Strada* wins Silver Lion Award, Venice.

1955   *Il Bidone* released but largely ignored.

1956   *Le Notti di Cabiria (The Nights of Cabiria)*. *La Strada* begins a three-year run in New York City, receives an Academy Award and a New York Film Critics Award for Best Foreign Film. Fellini's father dies.

1957   *The Nights of Cabiria* wins an Academy Award as Best Foreign Film; Giulietta Masina is voted Best Actress at Cannes.

1960   *La Dolce Vita* receives Best Film Award at Cannes.

1961   *La Dolce Vita* receives a New York Film Critics Award and a National Board of Review citation as Best Foreign Film.

1962   "The Temptations of Dr. Antonio" (part of a film anthology, entitled *Boccaccio '70*, produced by Carlo Ponti). (This book stops at this point.)

1963   8½ released and receives an Academy Award and a New York Film Critics Award as Best Foreign Film, as well as a National Board of Review Award as Best Foreign Language Picture.

1965   *The Nights of Cabiria* is adapted to a highly successful Broadway musical entitled *Sweet Charity*. *Giulietta degli Spiriti (Juliet of the Spirits)* released and receives a New York Film Critics Award as Best Foreign Film, a National Board of Review Award for Best Foreign Language Story, and a Golden Globe Award for Best Foreign Language Film.

1967   Suffers serious illness. He no longer works with Pinelli, Flaiano, and Rondi as his scriptwriters; turns instead to Bernardino Zapponi.

1968   "Toby Dammit" appears as part of a film anthology entitled *Histoires Extraordinaires/Tre Passi nel Delirio*, a French film production.

1969   *Fellini: A Director's Notebook* is produced for NBC-TV. *Fellini-Satyricon. Sweet Charity* becomes a movie, starring Shirley MacLaine.

1970   Fellini nominated for Academy Award as Best Director *(Satyricon). The Clowns.*

1971   *The Clowns* receives a National Board of Review citation as a Best Foreign Language Film.

1972   *Fellini's Roma.*

1974   *Amarcord* released and receives a New York Film Critics Award for Best Motion Picture, and an Academy Award and National Board of Review Award for Best Foreign Language Film. Fellini receives New York Critics Award for Best Direction.

1975   Fellini nominated for an Academy Award as Best Director *(Amarcord).*

1976   *Fellini's Casanova.*

1979   *Prova d'Orchestra (The Orchestra Rehearsal).* Nino Rota, who composed the music for all Fellini's films from *The White Sheik* through *The Orchestra Rehearsal*, dies.

1981   *La Città delle Donne (City of Women).* 8½ becomes the inspiration for the immensely successful Broadway musical, *Nine.*

1983   *La Nave Va.*

1

Fellini, Italian Neorealism, and the Contours of Vision

Fellini's predirectorial schooling in film consisted largely of his collaboration with Roberto Rossellini—particularly in scripting *Rome, Open City* (1945), in scripting and directing parts of *Paisan* (1946), and in scripting and acting in *The Miracle* (1947). That collaboration, in turn, made Fellini a significant figure in the movement that has come to be called "Italian neorealism" and that comprises films made by directors such as Rossellini, Luchino Visconti, and Vittorio DeSica roughly between the years 1943 and 1951. Fellini was greatly influenced by the spirit of neorealism, and a discussion of both the movement and Fellini's changing relation to it will help provide a useful introduction to Fellini's vision.

Defining neorealism is not a simple matter. There is a substantial gap between the theories of Cesare Zavattini, the movement's foremost apologist, and the films themselves. The difference tends to lie in the way in which "realism" is addressed. For Zavattini, realism entailed an extremely objective, reportorial method—one that approached the pure recording of reality without formative intrusion on the part of the director.[1] Yet all the major neorealist films were, in large part, fictional—clearly the result of imaginative shaping rather than mere mechanical replication. Recognizing this, scholars have begun to emphasize the fabricated, staged aspects of neorealist film as well as its documentary realism. They have also begun to point out how often neorealist filmmakers drew attention to the filmic and fictional nature of their work.[2] It has become clear that neorealism—in practice as opposed to theory—was not an attempt to deny imaginative creation and the role of the artist. It was an attempt to purify the imagination, redefine the task of art, through reconnection with the quotidian and concrete. As William Carlos Williams puts it in his preface to *Paterson:* "To make a start / out of particulars / and make them general, rolling / up the sum, by defective means—."[3] ("Defective" here affirms all the richness—including the crudity—of life, over the sterile perfection of entirely preconceived art.)

With the above as needed qualification, we can posit the following general goals of neorealist filmmaking: (1) to counteract the kind of illusions

Giulietta Masina, Fellini's wife of forty years, has been a crucial source of inspiration throughout his career. Here she introduces the character of Cabiria in a brief appearance in The White Sheik. *Courtesy: Museum of Modern Art/Film Stills Archive.*

promulgated by Italian films of the 1930s and 1940s: both the "White Tele-phone" escapist comedies which centered on the monied classes and were shot in highly artificial studio surroundings, and the propaganda films of the Mussolini regime; (2) to reveal the social and economic conditions of postwar Italy; leftist in spirit (without being abstractly ideological or polit-ical), neorealism sought to redirect Italian consciousness from bourgeois ideals to proletarian reality; (3) to awaken a new sense of human solidarity following the oppression and fragmentation of the Fascist period; (4) to develop a new sense of national cinematic identity, freed of dependence on Hollywood for either technique or romantic subject matter.

These goals implied certain methodological and technical choices, im-plemented with varying rigor depending on the filmmaker and the film. Common within neorealist films were: (1) a documentary openness toward life, designed to expose both artist and audience to what is there in the "real" world—and to destroy bourgeois preconceptions; "fact" or at least "reconstituted fact" was affirmed over make believe; (2) the use of real locations rather than sets, laborers and peasants rather than professional actors; (3) an emphasis on the commonplace and the common man over the exceptional; this denial of the "Hero" or "Great Individual" was a de-nial of leadership in favor of social equality, a reaction in part to the dicta-torial authority of Hitler and Mussolini; (4) the use of mise-en-scène over montage to preserve the integrity of reality and minimize its manipulation.

While Fellini's early films clearly share neorealism's opposition to bour-geois illusion, escapism, preconception, and authoritarianism (*The White Sheik* is almost a textbook study of these problems), the dissimilarities rather than the similarities between Fellini and neorealism initially seem most striking—especially from the perspective of the 1980s. The notion of a world "out there" waiting to be documented is far too static for Fellini. Particularly in his affirmative films, the world does not preexist, it is al-ways in the act of becoming. To stand removed from the process—to try merely to capture and analyze reality—is to remain one step behind. This becomes quite clear in the two Fellini films which feature journalists (Za-vattinian "neorealists" as it were): "A Matrimonial Agency" and *La Dolce Vita*. In each case, the main character suffers precisely because of his alienation from the act of living.[4]

Concomitantly, notions such as objectivity and detachment run counter to the Fellinian sense of love and engagement: "To hell with the objective, I've got to be in the middle of things. I must know everything about everyone, make love to everything around me. I don't like being just a tourist; I don't know how to be one. Rather, I'm a vagabond, curious about everything, entering everywhere, and all the time running the risk of being thrown out by the police."[5] Like Jake Barnes in Hemingway's *The*

Sun Also Rises, Fellini believes that growth results not from rational contemplation, knowledge at a distance, but from participation. As Barnes
put it: "I did not care what it was all about. All I wanted to know was how
to live in it. Maybe if you find out how to live in it you learned from that
what it was all about."[6]

As growth becomes increasingly possible for Fellini's characters, the sti-
fling socioeconomic conditions emphasized in neorealist film are seen in a
new light. Instead of serving as inescapable reality, they become trans-
formable. As Cabiria evolves beyond a material existence, she is able to
turn prostitution into genuine love. Her currency becomes not money but
spirit, her home not a little suburban box but the world at large. Even in
Fellini's less affirmative movies, the crucial human problems are no longer
materialist so much as spiritual. (This change in emphasis occurs not just
in Fellini but in the work of nearly all the directors who came of age during the neorealist period. Luchino Visconti and Michelangelo Antonioni
are the most obvious examples. But even Vittorio DeSica and Alberto Lattuada shifted their focus dramatically in later years with films such as *The
Garden of the Finzi-Continis* and *A Dog's Heart.*)

By the time Fellini gets to 8½, life transformed into imagination has
almost entirely replaced "primitive" reality even as the starting point of
his work. This is not a form of escape or rejection—just an acknowledgment that as people develop their powers of intelligence, "reality" becomes not brute fact but value: experience informed and evaluated by
mind. As Fellini's main characters become more imaginative, they come
to resemble less and less the "common man" prized by Zavattini. Cabiria,
for example, is genuinely exceptional in her capacity for creative experience. Yet she does not become a "hero" ("heroine") in the negative sense
of being separate, superior, dominant. In fact, her true genius and originality lie in her ability to become vitally related to everyone—"demo-
cratic" in the richest of ways. Individuation, which is a crucial dimension
of all Fellini's affirmative films, is never individuation *from,* it is always
individuation *in* and *through.* It leads to greater harmony, higher forms of
engagement. As Fellini himself has put it: "a person who really finds himself can insert himself into the collectivity with more freedom, more force
and confidence, precisely because he has found his individuality."[7]

Though in matters of emphasis, subject matter, and method, Fellini
and the neorealists seem to diverge almost to the point of radical opposition, their underlying kinship reasserts itself if we view them in terms of
fundamental commitments and motivating spirit. Both are bound by a
dedication to accuracy, faithfulness, and accountability. While neorealism
may have been more concerned with the authenticity of observation, Fellini is equally concerned with the validity of creation. The neorealists seek
to be true to the way things are, while Fellini seeks to be true to the way

things can be transformed. His accountability is to the truth of imagination; he is, as he has said, "a liar, but an honest one" (FF, 49).

In keeping with this (to move for a moment beyond the scope of this study) when Fellini moves into films that center entirely on art, he also hearkens back to his neorealist heritage by seeking to make "documentaries." He refers to his *Satyricon* as the "documentary of a dream," and in *The Clowns* and *Roma*—both of which are films about filmmaking—a principal motivating impulse is to "record" the history of the clown and the significance of Rome. Of course, in each case the documentary approach is, for reasons suggested above, found wanting. Nonetheless, it seems that Fellini compensates for his journey entirely beyond conventional realism by reapplying the documentary, verist goals of neorealism to his explorations of art and creativity.

Both Fellini and the neorealists are vitally concerned with the transformation of consciousness. The neorealists thought they could effect it by showing the negative consequences of war, Fascism, and bourgeois ideology. (They assumed the audience would draw the appropriate conclusions.) Fellini, instead, *enacts* transformation. Though this is particularly true of his later work (8½ through *Roma,* and *City of Women*), it begins to happen with *The Nights of Cabiria* and *La Dolce Vita.* Fellini enables—in fact requires—the audience to participate in the process of creative change in order to derive the kind of knowledge-through-participation mentioned above. His sense of the artist as one who offers models of transformation is suggested by his remark: "The important thing for man is to hang on, not to let his head droop but to keep looking up along the tunnel, perhaps even inventing a way of salvation through fantasy or willpower, and especially through faith. For this reason I think that the work of the artist is really needed today" (FF, 158).

Like the neorealists, Fellini is passionately dedicated to human solidarity. All his films are "love stories" in the profound sense of advocating such solidarity. In speaking of *La Strada,* he has described his concern with community and brotherhood in a way that applies not only to the story of Gelsomina and Zampanò but to all his work: "Our trouble, as modern men, is loneliness, and this begins in the very depths of our being. . . . Only between man and man, I think, can this solitude be broken, only through individual people can a kind of message be passed, making them understand—almost *discover*—the profound link between one person and the next" (FF, 61).

Fellini is motivated by the same quest for openness (the precondition of love and solidarity) that lay at the heart of neorealism. Zavattini has identified this quest in words which seem to undercut or at least qualify his insistence on objectivity: "to exercise our poetic talents . . . we must leave our rooms and go, in mind and body, out to meet other people . . .

This is a genuine moral necessity."⁸ And Fellini, in his oft-quoted description of neorealism, has accurately pinpointed openness as *the* defining characteristic of the movement: "For me neorealism is a way of living without prejudice and a means of liberating oneself completely from bias; in short, a way of facing reality without preconceived ideas."⁹

In his later work, Fellini's efforts to minimize preconception and "prejudice" are reflected in casting methods which are quite consistent with the neorealist ethic. Instead of trying to force stars and professional actors into fixed roles, he opens his office to hundreds of people—often redefining his narratives in terms of new faces and adding characters on the basis of the people he encounters. In effect, he creates his films largely from the raw material of people, a process documented in *Fellini: A Director's Notebook*. (See also *FF*, 103–5.)

This need to be free of prejudice, of fixed ideas and categories, of habits that blind one to the world, is in the largest sense a desire for renewed vision, recovered authenticity. It is in this, perhaps, more than anything, that Fellini and neorealism most fully conjoin. Each is engaged in a revolution against disabling tradition, institutionalization, and false consciousness. Fellini, in addressing this aspect of his work, could well be speaking for any neorealist filmmaker in the 1940s: "Doubtless a motif returns incessantly in my films, and it is the attempt to create an emancipation from conventional schemes . . .; that is to say the attempt to retrieve an authenticity of life rhythms, of life modes, of vital cadences, which is opposed to an inauthentic form of life. There, I believe, is the idea that is found in all my films" (*K*, 178–79).

As our discussion of Fellini and neorealism makes quite clear, Fellini's work emerges from a deeply felt sense of human responsibility, which influences his sense of himself, his art, and the role of the artist. Once asked about his greatest fears, Fellini replied: "The fear of falling, of growing too heavy. There is a vertical line in spirituality that goes from the beast to the angel, and on which we oscillate. Every day, every minute carries the danger of losing ground, of falling down again toward the beast."¹⁰ Fellini's art is, above all else, a struggle to overcome the dangers of falling. It is committed to the transcendence of gravity, of matter, of all that weighs down the spirit. It is an attempt to envision man's journey beyond the beast. At its best, it dreams Fellini and us anew, in a shared revolution of sensibility that brings us somewhat closer to the angels: "It is the no-man's land . . . the frontier between the world of the senses and the suprasensible world, that is truly the artist's kingdom" (*FF*, 154).

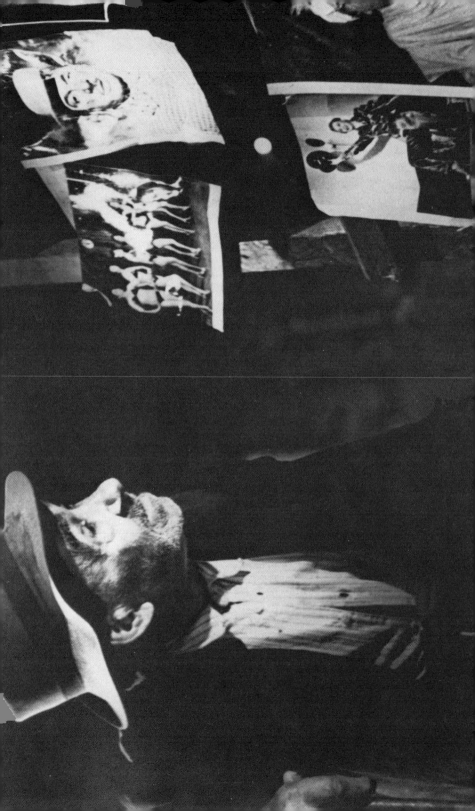

2

Variety Lights

Variety Lights (1950) was Fellini's first major directing venture. (The title refers to the lights of the "variety" or vaudeville theater.) Though the film was co-directed by Alberto Lattuada, it contains much that is discernibly Felliniesque. Moreover, Fellini himself has expressed a strong sense of authorship in discussing the film: "For *Variety Lights* I wrote the original story, wrote the screenplay, and chose the actors. Moreover, the film recalls some worn-out routines I saw presented by a vaudeville troupe with Aldo Fabrizi. . . . I can't remember exactly what I directed or what [Lattuada] directed, but I regard the film as one of mine."[1]

The Central Pattern

The film opens with a shot of a town clock, as a bell tolls the time. Quickly, the camera tilts down to pick up the image of an aged hunchback who leads the camera to a display, outside a theater, advertising Checco's show within. Suddenly, the camera is inside, watching the show from a distance—then from close up. Just as suddenly, it is up on stage, looking out at the audience from the point of view of a performer. It has become, in effect, a member of Checco's troupe—as caught up in make-believe as he.

Here the twin poles of the film are established: a world ruled by convention (clock time, bells) and physical determinism (the age and deformity of the hunchback), and a world of escape, of "freedom," where one can forget the constraints of reality. Moreover, the triumph of make-believe is something that will recur in each of the film's narrative processes: the geographical progression from the provinces to Rome, the growth of Liliana from a child of the provinces to a soubrette in Parmesani's Revue, and the struggle of Checco, via Liliana, to break away from Melina and his troupe and pursue a variety of artificial "lights" or ideals.

7

Discontent with reality leads to escape into fantasy in Variety Lights.
Courtesy: Museum of Modern Art/Film Stills Archive.

From the Provinces to Rome

The provinces are presented largely as a world of physical activity (especially walking), physical needs and processes (hunger, thirst, eating, drinking), and physical environment (extreme heat, torrential rain, and so on). Moreover, in the provinces, the troupe remains bound by practical considerations: train timetables, performance schedules, expenses, contracts, business commitments. (This is not to say that Checco and company do not endlessly bemoan and try to avoid their environment and obligations.) In contrast, Rome is a world of "International Fantasy," to borrow the title of one of Checco's numbers. It is composed of artists' hangouts, decadent nightclubs, theatrical rehearsals and performances; and it is a gathering place for Bohemian artists from distant lands—uprooted and lost in a private, art for art's sake, vision. (The epitome of this is the Hungarian choreographer who, unable to communicate the "great significance" of her ballet to her dancers, reduces them all to stasis!) The culmination of the Roman phase is Parmesani's revue, where mechanized illusion and escapism rule supreme.

The Roman world traps Liliana and Checco in its web of fantasy. They lose the ability to relate to anyone in a real or direct way. Though each may leave Rome behind in body at the end, neither abandons the realm of absolute fiction it comes to signify.

Liliana

Liliana's quest from the very beginning is to abandon home, family, and personal ties and become part of Checco's world of make-believe. More precisely, her goal is to abandon any selfhood she might have and become a "Star": the creation or projection of other people's dreams. Consequently, her progression from reality to illusion is presented largely in terms of loss of identity. She is forced to rely entirely on males such as Checco, Conti, and Parmesani. She does little to develop her own talents so that her success might be at least partially a reflection of her capabilities. And she sacrifices the energy and independence she possesses early in the film to become a mere decoration in Parmesani's revue. Her growing objectification is suggested when she abandons her dress with her initial *L* on it, when Checco changes her name from Antonelli to "Lilli" for advertising purposes, and when she adopts a short, unflattering hairdo and begins wearing tailored suits midway through the film. In effect, she sacrifices her very image and femininity.

Liliana's loss of identity is accompanied by her growing separation from those around her. The first time we see her, she is in the midst of an audience, and through the early part of the film she has a remarkable ability to connect with people (in fact to *force* connections). At Parmesani's revue, however, she is high above her audience, and as the act concludes she withdraws still farther, to be covered by a curtain. In the final scene, she is far above Checco in her first-class train compartment, insulated by a fur coat that is far more ample than weather would demand.

Checco

Just as Liliana gets swept up by the dream of stardom, Checco gets captivated by his dream of Liliana. In this respect he resembles a later Fellini character, Dr. Antonio (also played by Peppino De Filippo), who becomes obsessed with the billboard image of Anita Ekberg. (See chapter 11.)

The nature of the Checco-Liliana relationship is suggested by their names. "Checco" has overtones of *cieco*—the Italian word for "blind"—and Checco clearly becomes blinded by his attraction to Liliana. (We should note that, while Liliana's name recalls the mythological Lilith, a symbol of lustful temptation, it is Checco's *own* susceptibility to delusion that turns her into a Lilith figure. She is far less to blame than he; Fellini is definitely *not* saying woman is the root of all evil!)

As the movie progresses, Checco stops seeing Liliana for what she is (an attractive young girl who might conceivably offer him love, beauty, sexual fulfillment) and begins turning her into a symbol of his own advancement. By the time he has arrived in Rome, she has become (in his mind) his ticket to fame, artistic acclaim, wealth, power, and so on. She also becomes his symbol of lost youth, which he feels he can recapture by possessing her.

As Fellini makes clear, Checco's penchant for falsification and illusion is largely an ego or "head" problem. He sets his head apart from his body by keeping the top button of his coat buttoned. He draws further attention to it by wearing a ridiculous beret. And Melina establishes quite early in the film, as she feels his forehead, that he has a sick or fevered head.

It is Checco's head that is emphasized at crucial moments in his abandonment of reality. It is awakened to Liliana when she first approaches him—poking him with an umbrella as he sleeps on a train. It is caught by her—both physically and psychologically—when she seizes it and kisses it at the lawyer LaRosa's mansion. It surrenders to her completely in a Roman *pensione*, as she fills it with visions of theatrical glory ("What success lies ahead! . . . In every theater [we] play in. With . . . my name this high . . . and yours too, in lights up on the marquee . . .").[2] Here, his capitulation is so complete he begins hallucinating—hearing the sound of applause as he moves off into the night. Finally, his head is blown entirely by Liliana, when she announces that she is leaving him and he passes out.

By the end of the film, though Checco is restored to conscious life, he is not cured.[3] In fact, in the final scene, he is lost entirely in pretense. He tells Liliana that he has become a great success. (The troupe's destination clearly undercuts this.) He pretends that his troupe includes a Viennese ballet. (There is no evidence whatsoever.) He tells Melina he loves her. (He immediately contradicts this by flirting with a young girl.) He pretends that the girl has initiated the conversation. (The opposite is the case.) And, in trying to impress her, he claims that he manages the troupe. (At best he is only a performer.)

In doing all this, Checco clings to—in fact, reasserts—all the illusions he had earlier associated with Liliana; success, artistic acclaim, and so on. The young girl now replaces Liliana as his symbol of youth, beauty, and love. Worst of all, there is no suggestion that Checco is able at this point to distinguish between reality and fiction. More egoistic and *cieco* than ever, he has turned all the world into a stage and himself into the main attraction.

Variety Lights provides a useful introduction to Fellini. Even the title, while referring principally to a world of illusion, also implies abundance, enlightenment, and art—those very things which will be of principal concern to Fellini, especially in his affirmative movies such as *The Nights of Cabiria*, *8½*, and *Juliet of the Spirits*. The problem of self-deception and illusion will be central to all Fellini's early, negative films and will exist as obstacles to growth even in the later movies. The problem of the alienated ego or head will confront all Fellini's major characters from Ivan and Wanda of *The White Sheik* through Snaporaz (*City of Women*).

On a technical level, though *Variety Lights* is relatively conservative in terms of cinematic style, the opening moments, in which the camera itself proves the most important "character," hint at the extraordinarily complex role the camera eye will come to play in Fellini's later films.

Finally, and perhaps most important, *Variety Lights* establishes the problem of growth as the crucial issue in Fellini's work. For all their failings, Checco and Liliana are trying to make life better for themselves. The struggle for self-realization—and the varying ability of characters to achieve it—is, above all else, the "Fellini story." It will also, in large part, be the story of this critical study.

3

The White Sheik

The White Sheik (1952), Fellini's first film as sole director, evolved from a script written by Michelangelo Antonioni which focused on the *fumetti—* immensely popular romantic comic strips whose illustrations were composed not of drawings but of photographs. Largely as a result of Fellini's reworking of the script and his directorial influence, the film is clearly identifiable as the product of his rather than Antonioni's imagination.

The White Sheik and *Variety Lights*

Much as the title of *Variety Lights* suggested that all its world was a theater, the title of *The White Sheik* suggests that all *its* world is cartoon. Despite differences in locale and characterization, both films assert the all-encompassing presence and problem of make-believe. (To some extent, locale is not all that different, since Rome is the headquarters of illusion in each.) Not only is the underlying problem the same, but the same basic processes recur. A male and a female character begin, in a sense, married to each other (strictly speaking, Checco and Melina were, at best, engaged). They are temporarily "divorced" as one of them pursues an ideal love. Then they reunite, inauthentically, when the ideal fails. Put another way, characters move from reality to fantasy, and when the *object* of fantasy is removed (Liliana for Checco, the Sheik for Wanda), they return to reality only to impose fantasy on it. Seen in this light, the final scenes of *The White Sheik* and *Variety Lights* are quite similar. Just as Checco lies about his success and claims to love Melina, Ivan and Wanda dissemble about their recent past, and Wanda decides that Ivan is now her "Sheik."[1]

There is, however, one significant difference. While Checco is completely self-satisfied in his dreamworld at the end of *Variety Lights*, Ivan is not. He remains troubled by the sense that something went wrong the day before. And though he is virtually forced to accept the fictive "solution" provided by Wanda, he ends the film in a state of puzzlement. In this respect, he serves as a link between the wholly accepting Checco and

Wanda marvels at the apparition of her secular deity: the White Sheik.
Courtesy: Museum of Modern Art/Film Stills Archive.

13

Moraldo of Fellini's next film, *I Vitelloni*, who will respond to the inauthenticity of *his* world with outright rejection.

As in *Variety Lights*, growing illusion is accompanied by loss of identity. This is even more pronounced in *The White Sheik* and is expressed largely through a seduction/"rape" motif. It is in the midst of a *fumetti* episode about mass rape that Wanda is seduced out to sea by the Sheik and stripped (in mind) of her identity as Ivan's new bride. (Significantly, Wanda is only known by "aliases" in the world of the Sheik: "Fatma"—the name she is given as a character in the episode—and "Passionate Doll," the pen name she adopts for the Sheik.) At the same time, while Ivan's relatives are watching the seduction-studded opera *Don Giovanni*, Ivan is at the police station having his identity dragged out of him and "killed" by a typewriter that sounds like a machine gun. The loss of identity culminates, of course, in the final scene when Wanda must, in effect, turn her relationship with Ivan into a *White Sheik* cartoon in order to preserve it.

Finally, as in *Variety Lights*, illusion is seen largely as a "head" or ego problem. Wanda is accurately diagnosed as having a headache that pills cannot cure. Ivan is, like Checco, both a hat fetishist and a supreme egotist. And like Checco, he "loses" his head (fainting) near the film's end. The sickness of the head is so severe (and comical) that Ivan and Wanda are united in an insane asylum just prior to the conclusion!

While *The White Sheik* addresses many of the same issues that appeared in Fellini's preceding movie, it does so in a more complex way. For instance, in *Variety Lights*, the issue of illusion or make-believe was pretty much restricted to the theatrical world which embodied it. In *The White Sheik*, however, it is extended both through and beyond the *fumetti* to include an entire Roman world of institutionalized authority—a world of (largely masculine) hierarchies epitomized by church and state.

The *fumetti* themselves subtly bear the influence and authority of the church. With their White Sheik "god" who descends from on high (he first appears, surrealistically airborne, in a swing), with episodes entitled "Sins of Damascus" and "Souls in Torment," with characters such as "Fatma" (cf. Our Lady of Fatima), they are Catholic mythology rudely transformed into romantic fantasy. Thus Wanda, in submitting to the world of the *fumetti*, is submitting in surrogate form to Catholicism. This helps "explain" her later submission to the overt Catholicism of the papal audience, St. Peter's, and Ivan's uncle. Present only implicitly in the *fumetti*, institutionalism is a blatant source of fantasy in Ivan's world. As Fellini has said: "while Wanda follows The White Sheik as her dream romantic hero, [Ivan] follows his own mythology, consisting of the Pope . . . *bersaglieri*, the nation, the king."[2] Through Ivan, Fellini—for the first time in his career—identifies institutional authority with abstraction, falsehood, and the destruction of individuality. Moreover, by seeing Rome as the seat of

"Institution," he prepares for later films such as *La Dolce Vita* and *Roma* in which he will see the eternal city not just as a source of distinctly Italian problems but as a center of illusion for all of Western civilization.

The Problem of Dependency

One of the greatest limitations of the film's characters is their extraordinary dependency. Always a problem among Fellini's provincial characters, it might be termed the "provincial dilemma." (Although *The White Sheik* takes place in Rome, Ivan and Wanda are only there for a two-day honeymoon, and in attitude and actions they are clearly children of the provinces.) Fellini himself, in discussing *Amarcord* (1974), has identified the problem as: "this remaining children for eternity, this leaving responsibilities for others, this living with the comforting sensation that there is someone who thinks for you (and at one time it's mother, then it's father, then it's the mayor, another time Il Duce, another time the Madonna, another time the Bishop; in short, other people)."[3]

Ivan's whole quest is for conformity and security within some fixed structure. He (even more than Wanda) lives in a world of uniforms: priests, nuns, boy scouts, soldiers, porters, policemen. He himself is always uniformed, as is his uncle. Their ever-present suit, tie, and hat make them soldiers in the army of Respectable Bourgeois Citizens.

Moreover, all the major characters try to become or remain a child in some sort of family unit. Ivan's activity in the film is little more than a sustained search for the Father—his uncle and the pope being the two primary embodiments of that parental role. Wanda initially seeks inclusion in the "family" comprised by the crew making the *White Sheik* cartoon—a group presided over by a clearly paternal/patriarchal director. When that does not work, she settles for inclusion in Ivan's extended family. Ivan's uncle, of course, is a child within the family of the Vatican, and he too is off to see the Father (*Il Papa*) at the end. Even the White Sheik is revealed to be nothing more than a child when he and Wanda return to shore and he must answer to his "parents"—the director and the Sheik's maternal wife.

The characters' inability to grow beyond childish dependency lies at the center of one of the film's major recurring patterns: "break out" followed by "cop out." At the beginning of the film, Ivan and Wanda are (potentially) in the process of getting free of the provincial world of their immediate families. Shortly thereafter, Wanda breaks away from her restrictive relationship to Ivan and, in so doing, breaks beyond Rome to Fregene. The White Sheik momentarily forsakes his director and his marriage as he abducts Wanda in a sailboat. Ivan repeatedly deserts his extended family as he tries to conceal and solve the problem of Wanda's disappearance.

Ivan and Wanda leave their immediate families, however, only to join another at the film's end. Wanda's break out ultimately lands her in an insane asylum, where she capitulates to Ivan's obnoxious authority ("You have five minutes to get dressed. I don't want to hear anything now. First comes the honor of the family. . . . Get dressed right away" [*ES*, 194]). The White Sheik ends his adventure a cowed, repentant little boy. And Ivan breaks away only to rely on other parental figures—the police commissioner, a motherly prostitute, the authorities at the insane asylum— and only to return to uncle and *Il Papa* at the end.

The Fraudulence of Marriage

One of the ways in which *The White Sheik* addresses both fantasy and childishness is by demystifying marriage. In the course of the film, this noble institution is revealed to be little more than disguised alienation—a fiction and a dependency relation which covers for the fact that characters cannot truly communicate. This is discernible even among secondary characters such as Ivan's aunt and uncle and the White Sheik and Rita. But it is most evident in the relationship between Ivan and Wanda. The first thing they do upon reaching the hotel is lose each other. Then, Ivan yells orders and reads his appointment book while Wanda dreams abstractedly of pursuing the Sheik. Their honeymoon, if such it can be called, consists of entirely dissimilar experiences which leave them with even less in common by the end than they had at the beginning. As they move toward papal authentication of their wedding, they have become completely divorced in spirit. (Throughout their final conversation, Fellini never presents them in the same shot.)

Fellini's view of marriage was no doubt inspired at least in part by the harshness of Italian marriage laws at the time. An annulment—the only form of divorce acknowledged in Italy—was virtually impossible to get, leaving numerous people trapped in loveless relationships that were really divorces without sanction.

From here on in, marriage will be a recurrent motif for Fellini in his examination of the problem of love. In *I Vitelloni*, "A Matrimonial Agency," and *La Strada*, it will reappear as a false solution; in films such as *The Nights of Cabiria* and *Juliet of the Spirits* it will be expanded beyond institutional limits to become "marriage to everyone"—a relation based on individuation rather than dependency.

The White Sheik and "Institutional Aesthetics"

Dealing as it does with *fumetti*, which employ sets, actors, and photography to create a fictional world of words and images, *The White Sheik* can readily be considered a film about film. In fact, the film communicates its moral vision largely by emphasizing the limitations of the *fumetti* vis-à-vis cinema, and by establishing a divisive relationship (another "divorce") between words and images.[4]

The principal quality that separates the *fumetti* from movies is their stasis. Since they cannot capture live action, they must present a world that is fixed, permanent, absolute as it were, in its fictiveness. (Fellini emphasizes the killing of motion by having the actors in the *fumetti* freeze into stop-frame poses during the shooting of the rape sequence.) It is precisely this quest for permanence that we have identified as the "provincial dilemma" and as Ivan's and Wanda's problem. More precisely, it defines Wanda's inability—despite her seeming capacity for adventure—to get free of the rigid and linear Ivan. Though she wanders and wonders far more than he, it is only in search of something that can provide happiness ever after and free her from the responsibility of struggling moment to moment to live an open and self-creating existence. The papal-avuncular authority to which she submits at the end, though different in content from her *White Sheik* myth, is identical in terms of the finality and "salvation" it claims to guarantee.

Wanda's problem is also clarified through the irresolvable conflict between word and image. Words in the film are associated principally with the institutional world, the world of tradition and authority. (Words and their meanings are, to a large extent, inherited rather than created.) As a humble servant of that world, Ivan is a consummate word person, with his appointment book, his poetry, his repeated use of the phone, his elaborate explanation of Wanda's absence, and his reliance on her note to the White Sheik as his only piece of evidence. (To the extent that Ivan uses his eyes, it is either to read words or to stare bug-eyed at the world in utter incomprehension!)

Images, on the other hand, are associated with both direct and creative experience—with seeing things for oneself and with inventing one's own vision of things. They are, in short, associated with at least the possibility of individualized life. Wanda, accordingly, is much more sensitive to images than Ivan. Not only is she enthralled by the predominantly visual world of the *fumetti*, but she herself is a visual artist who draws a large sketch of the Sheik. In addition, especially early in the film, she tries to let her eyes get her where she wants to go. (Even her initial meeting with the Sheik is presented more as a visual apparition than as the result of any directions Wanda has received.)

Unfortunately, she lives in a world dominated by words. The *fumetti* episode is controlled entirely by the director and his megaphone; script proves far more important than image. The Sheik himself is all talk, no action. (He gets knocked silly by a sail boom when he tries to move from verbal to physical seduction.) She and her visual orientation end up victimized by language. The Sheik tells lies which humiliate her, and with her vision of love destroyed she must succumb to Ivan's absurd verbal demands at the insane asylum. The culmination of this, of course, is the final scene, where she closes her eyes to life and allows words ("You are my White Sheik" [*ES*, 197]) to take over, once and for all.

The victory of stasis over motion, word over image, institution over life, is confirmed in the film's very last shot. As the honeymooners and their entourage trot off toward St. Peter's, the camera sweeps up and away to the statue of an angel or saint high atop a roof, blessing a world from which it is completely removed. The statue is, of course, lifeless—a reduction of the individual to public monument. Moreover, its eyes are heavily lidded and appear to be closed. Not only that, the word *"Fine"* comes exploding out of the statue's head and takes over much of the screen—dictating to us what we should be able to figure out for ourselves. Hardly just an arbitrary conclusion, the final shot becomes an "icon" of a world ruled over by blind institutional authority. The statue is, in effect, Ivan's and his uncle's *"Papa"* and God.

Though Fellini's analysis of institutional "aesthetics" and his use of the *fumetti* are, in light of his later work, only mildly self-conscious in their examination of film, they do—like the role of the camera at the beginning of *Variety Lights*—display a sensitivity to the medium that will become consummately self-conscious in films like "The Temptations of Dr. Antonio" and 8½.

Before leaving *The White Sheik*, we must acknowledge the cameo appearance of Giulietta Masina in the role of Cabiria, a prostitute-companion of the woman who goes off with Ivan. A dynamic creature who is far less interested in prostitution than in spectacle and self-expression, she is the inspiration for *The Nights of Cabiria*, Fellini's first truly positive film and one of the most important of his early movies.

4

I Vitelloni

I Vitelloni (1953) was the first of Fellini's films to receive substantial critical acclaim. It was awarded the "Silver Lion" at the Venice International Film Show, and it became the first Fellini film to gain international distribution. The title of the film, which might be translated as "the overgrown calves" or "veals," was a term commonly used in the provincial world of Fellini's youth to describe males in their late twenties or thirties who refused to grow up—remaining unemployed, at home, and reliant on their (usually middle-class) families.

Like *The White Sheik* and *Variety Lights*, *I Vitelloni* is largely about characters who become accommodated to lives of illusion and social convention. At the same time, there is a more intensive analysis of the way society generates conformity. In fact, while Fellini's earlier films tended to emphasize individuals, *I Vitelloni* tends to pay equal attention to the subtle sociopolitical pressures that erode individuality and make submission to institutional illusion virtually inevitable. As a result, *I Vitelloni* is more deterministic than *Variety Lights* or *The White Sheik*—as well as more acceptable to those who favor an art of social realism.

The moral vision of *I Vitelloni* is built to a large extent on the seductive conservatism of the commonplace. We are given a typical situation to which characters react in perfectly normal ways. The events are *so* typical that we are inclined to accept them uncritically. Yet if we look closely, we discover that they (and our own inclination to accept) conceal and justify conservatism, the quest for security, fear of the "open air."

The thunderstorm at the film's beginning is a case in point. Everyone scurries for cover. Perfectly understandable, it would seem. Yet the storm and the mad dash for shelter help define a society which, in the largest sense, cannot face the elements—a society which has become what it is by protecting itself and shutting things out.

The world of the *vitelloni* is even more clearly defined by its response to the unwed Sandra's pregnancy. She herself reacts by fainting. Like

The vitelloni *and Sandra gather early in the film to hear the latest music from Rome (l. to r., standing: Leopoldo, an onlooker, Fausto, Sandra, Moraldo; seated: Riccardo, Alberto). Courtesy: Museum of Modern Art/Film Stills Archive.*

Checco and Ivan, she feels compelled to escape reality ("lose her mind") rather than deal with it. Moreover, her faint is a movie cliché or convention—emphasizing the fact that she is acting only in the most typical of ways. Worst of all, her tendency to avoid life is so pronounced that when she comes to, all she can say is, "I want to die. I want to die."[1]

Sandra's penchant for evasion is mirrored by Moraldo, who keeps telling his mother "It's nothing" (TS 13–14), and by the doctor, who orders the room cleared before disclosing his diagnosis. He never does, in fact, disclose his diagnosis, thus acknowledgment of the pregnancy remains suppressed until the following scene.

Consistent with their negative response to new life, the characters prove far more attuned to endings than beginnings. The Miss Siren contest celebrates not spring but the end of summer (a double ending in a sense). Leopoldo reacts to the thunder and lightning by predicting that it will be the end of the party. Just before Sandra faints, Moraldo remarks that it "looks like the end of the world" (TS, 11). And, at the beginning of the next scene, Fausto remarks that it is the end of the season.

Society never does treat Sandra's pregnancy *as* pregnancy. At first, it is dealt with only as a violation of convention. Then, through the institution of marriage, it is turned into a convention itself. The new is made to conform to the old and established; the living, as it were, is appropriated by the dead. As a result, even the wedding is an ending more than a beginning. It puts a *stop* to a socially unacceptable situation.

All this again seems quite normal. (It must have seemed particularly so at the time in which the film was made.) Yet the subtly self-serving conservatism that underlies the characters' actions is made clear when Fausto's father insists on marriage, not to provide a stable family environment for the child but to preserve his "honor" and that of Sandra's father.

A world that cannot live openly—that must turn life into convention—is, inevitably, incapable of love. In fact, it must turn *love* into convention—into symbols and objects that can be manipulated, kept at a distance, substituted for real involvement. The Miss Siren contest makes this clear. Love is reduced to the Female as Sex Object—and that object, in turn, is neutralized, "sterilized," by being put on a pedestal for all to see but no one to touch. (The fact that Sandra has indeed been touched is the ultimate affront to the repressive-projective psychology of the Beauty Pageant.) Moreover, the love object herself has no autonomy. She has (we are told) been pressured by her mother into entering the contest. She is insulted and interrupted (albeit playfully) by Riccardo when she is about to make her "acceptance speech." She is led, pawed, pulled, and hemmed in by her admirers. And by the end of the scene she is prostrate in the care of a doctor whose severe patriarchal image introduces the world of male authority which will repeatedly assert its control during the film.

The absence of love as anything other than convention is, of course, evident in the marriage of Sandra and Fausto. They are never seen together before the wedding. (Fausto spends the evening of the contest pursuing another woman.) They are united not out of love but out of social and paternal pressure. (Fausto tries to run away but is bullied by his father into facing up to his responsibilities.) As in *The White Sheik*—but in a much less comic way—marriage comes to deny rather than to promote true interaction.

As the movie progresses, the inability of characters to free themselves from social constraints remains clearest in the Sandra-Fausto relationship. Once Sandra is neutralized in the opening scenes—both by her world and by her own implicit "death wish"—she comes to embody social convention herself: playing the traditional roles of dependent wife and mother, and failing to make a life of her own. Fausto, on the other hand—like Wanda—tries to escape the institutionalized life of marriage. However, again like Wanda, he escapes only into new and greater dependency relationships. He never grows up, and when Sandra temporarily deserts him, he discovers how reliant he is on her. They end up reconciled out of weakness rather than strength, need rather than love, much like the characters of Fellini's preceding movies.

The way the reconciliation comes about reveals just how dependent Fausto has become, not just on Sandra but on the conventional world she has come to represent. First of all, unable to find Sandra on his own, he visits the town's religious articles shop and places himself in the hands of Signor Michele. As an authoritarian figure, linked to Catholicism through his work, Michele is *the* supreme embodiment of convention in the film. (He also is trapped in a marriage of convenience and need.) Moreover, as Fausto's former boss, he has already been associated with Fausto's forced capitulation to social order. Fausto's return to Michele's authority marks a second, far more absolute, capitulation.

Second, Michele takes Fausto to Fausto's father, who soundly thrashes him as the penitential condition of reunion with Sandra. This scene recapitulates the prewedding encounter in which Fausto is bullied into marrying Sandra, but here the authoritarianism of the father is even more pronounced.

Finally, the Sandra to whom Fausto reconciles himself has become an authority figure. She is a parent, not a wife, and Fausto submits as a child, not a husband:

Sandra (*severe*). . . . If you get me mad another time, I'll do just like your father. Even worse!

Fausto stops and smiles at her. For the first time he sees Sandra in a new light. She is no longer the little girl who suffered every wrong, submissive and humble, playing the role of the victim.

Sandra (*decidedly*). I'll beat the hell out of you!
Fausto looks at her again.
Fausto (*smiling*). That's the way I like you! (*TS*, 129–30)

"Youth fades away, love fades away" (*TS*, 100). So says Sergio Natale during a stage monologue, and his words capture a crucial reality, not just in the Sandra-Fausto relationship, but in the lives of all the characters as they continue to substitute objects, symbols, and illusions of relatedness for real involvement. At its most mundane, this consists of relating to one another merely to borrow a cigarette, a light, money, or some other mediating article (another instance of Fellini using the commonplace to sketch social evasions and conventions). On a more profound level, Alberto replaces love with slavish dependence on his sister, Leopoldo supplants communication (his urge to be a dramatist) with worship of the washed-up Natale, the town as a whole feigns community through a carnival where everyone is disguised and/or drunk, and Catholicism reduces itself to the artifacts bought and sold at Signor Michele's emporium.

Consistent with this is the theft of the wooden angel. Here, paradoxically, a symbol of spirit becomes the means only for Fausto to avenge the fact that he has been fired, and the statue becomes the sole source of connection between Fausto and Michele, Fausto and Moraldo, and the two *vitelloni* and their world. Moreover, when the *vitelloni* entrust the angel to the mentally impaired Giudizio, who paws it reverentially, the angel comes to define a world where "love" is merely idolatry.

The culminative expression of this is Natale's revue. After a series of maudlin routines, the revue presents a dancing girl (with whom Fausto later spends the night) dressed as the Italian flag. Society's symbol of love is no longer Sandra or Miss Siren, it is *Italia*. Her concluding number, which captivates the audience, suggests that love reduced to dependency, objectification, and illusion leads to the kind of patriotism that gave rise to Mussolini and Fascism.

In many ways the key figure in *I Vitelloni* is Moraldo. As his name suggests, he embodies the "mores" of his world. He repeats the phrase "It's nothing" five times within a few moments of the opening scene, making clear that, like everyone else, he is given to repression. Furthermore, in a more significant way than anyone else, he responds to Sandra's pregnancy in a conventional rather than a fully human way. He is Sandra's brother. Yet when she has regained consciousness and is lying on the floor in both physical and spiritual distress, he makes no effort to comfort her. Instead, he immediately begins to suspect "the worst" and to cast questioning glances at both Sandra and Fausto. Then, he leaves her on the floor and pursues Fausto to convey his concern with this disturbing violation of convention. (Though he has not yet become openly censorious, his very presence at Fausto's house is a judgment of sorts: a reminder to Fausto of his obligations.) Subtly, yet unmistakably, he can view Sandra and Fausto only as transgressors—not as sister and friend. Worst of all, it never crosses his mind to see the creation of new life in a positive way.

As the film progresses, Moraldo's mores harden into morality (his name becomes synonymous with the latter more than the former). His tendency to adopt a critical stance toward life becomes far more pronounced. His escapism and detachment (he is always stargazing or staring absently off into space) lead him to withdraw behind moral standards of right and wrong, to relate to people only in a spirit of judgment.

His quiet concern regarding Sandra's pregnancy becomes explicit criticism of Michele for firing Fausto. This is followed by a "righteous" act of vengeance, as he helps Fausto steal the wooden statue. (Here Moraldo is kin to Michele and Fausto's father, each of whom subscribes to a morality of retribution.) Next he wrongfully accuses Signore Michele (to Sandra) of making advances to Fausto. Then he becomes uncompromisingly critical of Fausto for his evening with the dancing girl. His behavior as he tries to make Fausto feel guilty outside the woman's hotel prompts Fausto to ask: "Want to *preach* to me? Is that why you waited?" (subtitles). Finally, after Sandra has run away with the baby, he renounces Fausto as a coward and tells him, in effect, that he would not care if Fausto were dead.[2] By this point, Moraldo is unable to relate to life in anything other than negative and moralistic terms. Consequently, his departure in the final scene becomes his conclusive moral "statement" about his friends, his town, his life to this point, his world.

Moraldo is not presented unsympathetically by Fellini. His growing inclination to censure is, like so much in the film, normal and understandable. What it serves to do, however, is illuminate a world in which all life is reduced to morality—an extremely authoritarian form of convention. Morality, in fact, becomes the final and most destructive love-surrogate as human relations become arbitrated in terms of how people should and should not behave.

(The morality of detachment, judgment, censure, guilt, and punishment is, of course, that of Catholicism. However, Fellini is careful not to identify it solely or even principally with the church. His point instead is to show how thoroughly such morality has come to infect every aspect of provincial existence, even the most secular.)

Because Moraldo's decision to leave town is merely another form of rejection and escape, rooted in precisely the kind of mentality that has created all the problems in the film, it fails to solve anything. His departure is yet another end, not a beginning. This is strongly suggested when his train begins to leave the station and he looks out the window, ahead, presumably to the future. All he can see is a vision of the past: images of the other *vitelloni*, Sandra, and Sandra's child at home, in bed, asleep. Devastated by a past he cannot leave behind, he slumps to a sitting position, eyes full of tears, and lowers his head to his hands. Thus concludes his visual presence in the film.

Moraldo's dead-to-the-world companions suggest the loss or denial of consciousness; the surrender to security, home, and family; the isolation; and the death-in-life that provincial existence fosters in the film. An even more saddening representation is provided by the film's brief concluding sequence—rightfully acknowledged as a "classic" among film endings.

Guido, a young, cheerful acquaintance of Moraldo who works at the railroad station, has followed Moraldo's train part way down the tracks. With Moraldo gone, he turns around and heads back.[3] He does a tightrope walk, with arms extended, on one of the rails; receives a paternal pat on the head from a uniformed male; slips momentarily off the rail; quickly steps back on; and "dies" when a freeze frame—the only one ever to conclude a Fellini film—immobilizes his image in a pose both birdlike and cruciform.

Among other things, this concluding sequence: (1) reduces Guido's helical dance down the street the first time he appeared to a mere "toeing of the line"; (2) confines Guido's impulse for flight to a straight and very narrow path; (3) entraps Guido in a world of male authority and uniformity (Guido, too, is uniformed); and (4) replaces the arm-in-arm linkage of the *vitelloni* that we have seen more than once in the film with Guido's arms that touch no one. In so doing, the sequence finalizes the victory of static convention over vital individuality and the reduction of love to paternal authority. The freeze frame even implicates Fellini as a directorial "authority" who imposes a technical convention in order to kill the moving world of his film. By freezing the young Guido as a cruciform figure—a Christ symbol—the concluding image sacrifices the new to the old, the unique to cultural abstraction. It asserts once and for all that the world of *I Vitelloni*, in its hostility toward the new, can eventuate only in endings.

I Vitelloni and Fellini's Imaginative Development

The White Sheik was an advance over *Variety Lights* principally because it told the same story (characters submitting to illusion) with greater sophistication. *I Vitelloni* is an advance over both because, in addition to telling the same story through Fausto, Sandra, Leopoldo, Alberto, and Riccardo, it tells a new and crucial one through Moraldo: the *rejection* of illusion and convention. Though Moraldo himself does not gain by it, his attempted breakout starts Fellini's imagination on the road to individuation. The false marriages that have provided a principal motif in Fellini's first three films give way to "divorce" or uprootedness as Fellini's characters get beyond town and family and move toward Rome and the struggle to make it in a new environment. Mindless conformity gives way to alienation, and though this marks a tragic phase in Fellini's work (the end of *Vitelloni* offers the first significant hint of tragedy), it also means that his characters are becoming more unique, dynamic, and independent.

I Vitelloni is also the first Fellini film in which something positive asserts itself. Sandra's pregnancy affirms, metaphorically even more than biologically, the possibility of something new and authentic being born amid rigid social custom. The emergence of authenticity accounts for the shift in focus in *Vitelloni* from characters who accept convention to a social order that must repress and destroy something that is not conventional. The sense of promise and potential destroyed is what gives *I Vitelloni* its ultimate tone of sadness.

The element of promise and authenticity is present not just through Sandra's pregnancy, but through the character of Moraldo. Though we have tended to emphasize how and why he ends up negatively, there is much to recommend him. He is youthful, attractive, and sensitive. Moreover, in the opening scene, before he discovers Sandra's pregnancy, he is curious, affable, and able to take boyish pleasure in what is going on. Unfortunately, because he is immediately thrust into a situation in which conventional morality dictates his responses, his curiosity and openness quickly erode and, as our discussion of his departure would suggest, are gone by the film's end.

I Vitelloni also marks an advance for Fellini in terms of narrative technique. There is much greater complexity in characterization—evident not only in the increased number of major figures but in the subtle narrative function of the five *vitelloni*. Each ultimately comes to "specialize" in a single facet or power of personality: Fausto is the physical or animal power, Alberto the emotional or "feminine," Leopoldo the intellectual (pseudo though it is), Moraldo the institutionalized conscience or Superego. Moreover, Riccardo—who is played by Fellini's brother and who resembles the director—suggests Fellini's imaginative presence in the film. Unfortunately, living in a repressive and divisive world, he remains subsidiary and becomes even less important as the film progresses. It is only at the beginning that he can serve as the town's unifying voice and expressive force and manifest a spontaneity, responsiveness, and generosity of spirit that bespeaks imaginative life.

Fellini's use of characters as personality fragments further emphasizes the disconnection of the *vitelloni's* lives. It reveals yet again the lack of wholeness on the part of each. And, it enables Fellini to turn the film into a process of dismemberment. As the individual *vitelloni* are cast off, one by one, the "whole person," which the five potentially comprise, is destroyed, leaving Moraldo (morality/convention) as the sole remnant.

Nowhere is Fellini's growing artistry and subtlety more apparent than in his use of voice-over narration. In a world where inner harmony and relatedness are impossible, the narrator constitutes *imposed* harmony. Describing himself as a composite of the *vitelloni*, he is a substitute for Riccardo, a false, external "imagination." In a world of authority and control, he becomes the god (a disembodied male voice) to whom the characters and their world owe their existence. (He is similar in this respect to Fellini in his role as directorial authority, who imposes a freeze frame on the film's final image.) In a world of convention, he—like the freeze frame, Sandra's faint, and the "happy-ending" reconciliation of Sandra and Fausto—is just one more commonplace cinematic trick or device. Since he is the presumed author of all that we see, his presence confirms that everything in the film is born of mere storytelling convention.

5

"A Matrimonial Agency"

"A Matrimonial Agency" (1953) is one of several episodes in a neorealist film anthology produced by Cesare Zavattini and entitled *Love in the City* (*Amore in Città*).[1] Zavattini himself contributed an episode as did Antonioni, Lattuada, and Dino Risi.

Zavattini intended *Love in the City* to fulfill his neorealist notions of film as objective reportage: "In [*Love in the City*] real events were to be related, with the real-life characters in those events talking about themselves in front of the camera, without the interference of a director. It was to be, purely and simply, a documentary."[2] Refusing to embrace Zavattini's aims, Fellini made the most obviously fictional of *Love in the City's* many episodes. Moreover, the nature of Fellini's story subtly subverts the intent of Zavattini's project. Though Fellini makes his main character a reporter (providing surface consistency with the project), he makes the reporter's professional detachment the symptom of profound moral blindness.

As a story of mediation and detachment, "A Matrimonial Agency" has much in common with *I Vitelloni*. It also focuses—as do all Fellini's preceding movies—on dependency, convention, and the absence of love. All three are suggested by the role of the agency: a commercial institution on which people rely to provide marriages based on anything but love. The extent to which love is compromised is implied by the agency's striking resemblance to a brothel. It is presided over by a "madam" (the "Signora"), guaranteed protection by the police (Attilio, the Signora's associate, is an ex-cop), and set up to procure young ladies for males.

In terms of narrative and moral structure, "A Matrimonial Agency" consists of two interrelated tales: the awakening of sensitivity on the part of the reporter through his encounter with Rosanna, and the growth to adulthood. Both are traditional, positive stories—narrative clichés as it were—which extend the controlling power of convention into the realm of the reporter's storytelling art. However, the positive nature of each is subverted by the film's overall moral vision. The reporter's awakening is revealed to be mere self-delusion, and he grows to maturity by losing the ability to relate to others—especially Rosanna. The two stories merge into a single process of "divorce" and "*adult*-eration" in which everything potentially unitive and childlike is destroyed.

Early on, the world of the film is populated principally by children. The most important character, aside from the reporter himself, is a young girl who leads him to the agency's doorstep. The adults who appear are ineffectual and seem to exist largely as support systems for the young (e.g., mothers caring for their babies).

Not only are children everywhere in evidence, but the film conveys an atmosphere of childhood. The action is fluid and irrational as children magically appear, weave their way through the labyrinthine passages of the apartment building, then disappear. Childhood intuition is a major force as the reporter's young guide realizes that he is looking for the agency without being told so. Even the reporter has many of the positive qualities of a child: openness, curiosity, spontaneity. Despite his journalist's singularity of purpose, he remains largely in tune with everything around him.

Of course, coexisting with the image and character of the reporter is his voice-over narration, describing in the past tense what he earlier underwent. Whereas the character represents the reporter when he was a visible and concrete figure, capable of direct involvement, the narrative voice represents what the character has become as a result of his experiences: invisible, distanced, capable only of disembodied re-creation. The voice is, in effect, the reporter as adult. Moreover, since it is the reporter as narrator (not as character) who is responsible for the story being told, the reporter as character, even at his most childlike, is at the mercy of adulthood. This means that though the childhood phase of the film does not entail any division between adult and child within the reporter as character (such a division will later emerge), a split does exist on the level of narrative structure. Division and *adult*-eration are thus built into the film from the outset.

Once the reporter is led to the matrimonial agency, a radical change occurs. Most obviously, children are left behind. The only reasonable facsimile is Attilio, who conducts the reporter from the agency's waiting room (where children are still in evidence) to the childless world of the Signora. As a threshold figure Attilio is both man and child. Though middle-aged, he is restless and incessantly talkative (like most children in Fellini's films)—and given to cutting out paper figures!

As children are left behind, things become static, segmented, controlled, and concrete reality gives way to abstraction. All this is epitomized by the Signora, who replaces the reporter's vibrant, intuitive young guide as the principal female figure. Authoritarian and coldly efficient, she works out of an office whose isolation contrasts sharply with the populous, connective hallways predominant earlier. Inside her office, people are replaced by lifeless representations (a tailor's mannequin, a bust, photographs); the experiential world is replaced by a globe of the world; and speech (direct communication) is replaced largely by writing.

Instead of the vital interaction (true "marriage") of affectionate individuals so evident among the children, we now have "Marriage" with a capital *M:* a contractual agreement rooted in cold, abstract, motive (money on the part of the agency; social propriety and financial security on the part of clients). Marriage, as we have seen so often in Fellini's early work, has become the very opposite of intimacy. (Indicatively, the Signora, despite her name, shows no signs of having a husband, and she and Attilio—the "parents" as it were of the agency—have no real relationship.)

At this point, the split between child and adult, which has been implicit all along in the narrative structure, becomes explicit in the activity of the reporter as character. He enters the Signora's office as a "child," curious and unarmed with any rational explanations for his presence: "As I sat down before the agency woman, I suddenly realized I had forgotten to make up a story, a reason for being there."[3] His sudden realization marks the beginning of adulthood, motive, calculation, and so forth. Nevertheless, though he submits to the adult world by providing a "reason for being there," his explanation (that he is a doctor representing a werewolf who thinks that marriage might cure him) is patently childish. Moreover, the doctor-werewolf twosome he invents reflects the kind of division he is undergoing. As someone capitulating to the adult, institutional world, he takes on the role of doctor. But as someone reluctantly abandoning the world of childhood, he temporarily salvages the child within through the werewolf—a figure anathema to rationalized adult society. (Of course, by this point in the film, the "child" can only exist in negative form, as something abnormal, perverse.)

Though the werewolf tale is largely divisive, it also embodies some potential for unity, through the urge of the lycanthrope to marry. However, this urge—and the lycanthrope itself—are ultimately denied, leading to a conclusive victory of adult over child and the destruction of unity on every level.

This is reflected principally in the failed relationship between the increasingly adult reporter/"doctor" and the childlike Rosanna. Part of the blame lies with Rosanna. She is the least vital of the prominent female figures in the film. (As the adult world gradually gains ascendency, vibrant femininity dies off.) And she embodies childhood not as a stage of promise, but as mere arrested development.

Most of the blame, however, lies with the reporter. He functions more and more as a voice of reason and conventional order, discouraging Rosanna ever more explicitly from marriage to his lycanthrope client. In so doing, he destroys the last traces of childhood in the film. He shatters Rosanna's optimism and hope—a diminished but still valuable form of the openness and dynamism of the earlier children. Even more important, he repudiates the werewolf figure he invented, insisting that the werewolf is not suitable for marriage. He thus negates the child half of the werewolf/ doctor division within him. At the same time, he repudiates both the tale and the childlike inventiveness that gave birth to it.

In killing off the werewolf, the reporter eliminates the principal basis for communication between himself and Rosanna. As the film concludes, he makes no attempt to be even courteous, much less kind. He abruptly shuts off conversation ("forget all about it") as they sit by the roadside in the country. He neither walks with her as they return to his car nor holds the door for her, as he prepares to drive back to the city. On the return trip, he does not speak a single word to her. When they arrive in the city, he drops her in the middle of a busy intersection—lacking even the decency to pull over to the curb—then he drives off alone.

Even more revealing than the reporter's visible activity is his concluding voice-over narration:

We returned to the city in silence. I wanted to say something to her. Not to justify myself or apologize, but something that would really help. I wanted to tell her to have more confidence in herself. To open her eyes to the countless possibilities that life presents each day. But I knew it would all sound like a lot of hot air, useless. Her immediate problems, her daily needs—these would have seemed to her the only real and important things. So I said nothing. When we parted, I sincerely wished her good luck.

This "sincere wish" is never presented in the film. Much more important, the reporter's words are nothing but conventional journalistic condescension, delivered in a tone of smug self-congratulation. They assert an absolute division between intention ("I wanted to tell her") and action ("So I said nothing"), carrying Fellini's subversion of neorealist "objectivity" and distance to its logical extreme. Finally, they proclaim the death of *meaningful* communication and, in their smugness, they reveal that the reporter—and his tale of moral awakening—are as divorced from reality, as lost in illusion, as the characters at the end of *The White Sheik* and *Variety Lights*.

Though a short and largely neglected movie, "A Matrimonial Agency" proves quite important in Fellini's career. By rejecting neorealism (at least as it was viewed by Zavattini), he asserts his independence from the principal cinematic tradition or "convention" which he had inherited. (He performs a Moraldo-like act of rejection, though with far more positive results.) This opens the way for a new and more personal kind of cinema, evident as early as his next movie, *La Strada*.

"A Matrimonial Agency" is also an advance in characterization. Although the reporter (unlike Moraldo) fails to experience real crisis or disillusionment, he is the first Fellini character to use his powers of invention in a way that gives form to the problems in and around him. Moreover, his voice-over is more creative than that of the narrator in *I Vitelloni*. Whereas the latter seemed merely to be recording past events, the former shapes them, at least to the extent of trying to tell a story of maturation and self-discovery.

In addition, the reporter is the first fully uprooted, hence potentially independent, Fellini figure. Moraldo got from the heart of town to the outskirts; the reporter, in a sense, has taken the train all the way to Rome. (In his extreme detachment, he is a "Moraldo in the City"—the title, incidentally, contemplated by Fellini for the project that turned into *La Dolce Vita*, another story about an alienated reporter.) He has no provincial past (Rosanna substitutes for it in the film). He has no family, no community, no friends, and his home is a single small unshared room. In his aloneness he prepares the way for Zampanò and *Il matto* of *La Strada* and Augusto of *Il Bidone*. Though he, like them, proves unable to act creatively, he serves—as they will—to move Fellini's imagination toward stories of genuine independence and individuation.

6

La Strada

With *La Strada* (1954) we come to a landmark both in Fellini's career and in European film of the past thirty years. Though the film created controversy among Italian Marxists, who deplored its poetic (i.e., nonneorealist) style, it was enormously successful; enjoying a three-year run in New York City, receiving more than fifty international awards, and bringing Fellini his first Oscar. The film's historical importance seems equaled by its importance to Fellini himself. He has said: "*La Strada* will remain the crucial point in my life."[1] And, even twelve years after completing the film, he remarked: "*La Strada* is really the complete catalogue of my entire mythical world. . . ."[2]

Fellini's continued concern with conformity, mediation, and estrangement is reflected in the way the film's title relates to the story. A road is something already laid out—a civilized "convention"—which encourages everyone to travel the same restrictive route. (The railroad has similar significance in some of Fellini's preceding films.) The road is also a purely physical form of relatedness which comes, in *La Strada*, to be the only way people can connect in a world without love. Its capacity to separate eventually exceeds its ability to unite, and in failing to lead people to fulfillment, the road becomes an avenue to violence, death, abandonment, and alienation. Fellini's road is clearly different from Walt Whitman's *open* road, which expands beyond all physical limitation to become a comprehensive symbol of freedom and unification.[3]

One of the principal concerns in *La Strada* is the loss of potential, the elimination of creative possibility. A sense of loss is established right from the beginning with the reported death of Rosa—Gelsomina's sister whom Zampanò is seeking to replace. Though Rosa remains undefined, "unrealized" in the film, her name links her with a mandalic symbol of wholeness. She comes from a time in Zampanò's life when things unattainable in the present may still have been possible. She may well derive from that period when Zampanò acquired his marvelous "mobile home," which offers the promise of a rich and adventurous life. Whatever else she may be, she

Gelsomina's wide-open, sunburst eyes associate her brightness and intelligence with the life of an artiste *in* La Strada.

embodies something unrecoverable except in diminished form in the film. Her loss and Zampanò's inability to come to terms with it may well explain his brooding, repressive nature—his determination never to be vulnerable (again).

A sense of loss is present not only through Rosa but through the diminishment of all three of the film's major figures—Gelsomina, Il matto, and Zampanò—who are the most advanced characters to this point in Fellini's career. Gelsomina is the first Fellini figure capable of real growth. Her active intelligence and her ability to respond creatively to experience set her apart from the Checcos, Wandas, Moraldos, Sandras, and Rosannas that preceded her. Il matto is a superb artiste (violinist, high wire performer, clown) who uses his artfulness with great ingenuity to mask his loneliness and vulnerability. Zampanò, though he might seem terribly limited, is associated with a full range of positive human values: love (his relation with Rosa, his need for Gelsomina), creation and communication (his life as an artist), the "marriage" of home and profession (his van), as well as an active life on the road. Moreover, he surrounds himself with evocative symbols—an owl, snake, mermaid, and crossed swords—that bespeak an imagination struggling to express itself. Even his strong-man routine, the breaking of a chain with his pectoral muscles or "heart," is a metaphoric representation of his urge to free himself through love. It is the failure of Gelsomina, Il matto, and Zampanò to act out their positive impulses that makes La Strada such an intensely tragic film.

The narrative process of La Strada is (like that of "A Matrimonial Agency") one of "adult-eration." Gelsomina, the childlike naif, is brought by Zampanò into an adult environment of work, money, discipline, convention, and linear thought, and she is destroyed. Her life quickly becomes fragmented, polarized; she is forced to sacrifice her identity; and her intelligence is compromised to the point of madness.

In the opening sequence, Gelsomina is an image of childhood promise, and a figure wholly in tune with her natural surroundings. ("Gelsomina"—"jasmin"—is a shrub, and with a bundle of brushwood on her back, she looks like a moving bush.) Once she is summoned to her mother and to Zampanò, this marvelously natural creature enters the world of civilized structure, economic and social forms, control. Zampanò leans heavily against the stone post of a building. The wooden frame of a small boat appears next to Gelsomina's head. Money is introduced as we discover that Zampanò has in effect bought Gelsomina. (He also gives two children money to buy food.) Social propriety is emphasized as the children are ordered to say "thank you." Subtly, but most significantly, discipline and domination manifest themselves as Zampanò equates the education he intends to give Gelsomina with the training of dogs.

In effect, Zampanò represents the point at which nature and civilization meet. Moreover, as someone who will introduce Gelsomina to planned, rather than purely spontaneous, behavior (repetition, rehearsal, memorization, performance), he embodies a rudimentary form of civilized intelligence crucial to the awakening of Gelsomina's mind.

As soon as Gelsomina enters Zampanò's world, she drops her bundle of wood. Moreover, she immediately accepts adult forms and "grows up." She accedes to the deal between her mother and Zampanò. She bids a reverential farewell to the sea (an act of deliberation in contrast to her earlier pure impulsiveness). She identifies goals (becoming a singer, dancer, and provider for the family). Then she breaks her childhood ties with home, even disregarding her mother's sudden plea that she stay. She runs toward Zampanò's van—the most sophisticated product of civilization thus far—and she enters the road and the life of directedness, teleology, and social constraint which it bespeaks. Sold into a world of domination, Gelsomina suffers the erosion of her individuality and freedom from the moment she leaves the purely natural world. Moreover, from the perspective of conformist society, her individuality is seen as something "strange," something negative, as her mother suggests by saying: "*it's not your fault* that you are not like the others."[4] In addition, as a commodity and tool in the service of Zampanò, Gelsomina is forced to derive her identity from him (in fact, her face only becomes visible at the moment she is brought into his presence). Accordingly, her departure with him and her life of adventure and opportunity are strongly qualified by images of effacement. As she waves good-bye, she covers her face with her cape. Then, after she has mounted Zampanò's van, she disappears behind its black curtains. By the scene's end she is, in effect, obliterated.

Seen in its largest context, the opening sequence implies a world in which civilization cannot productively assimilate the natural. It must appropriate and dominate. What might have been creative evolution becomes opposition and conflict, which are only resolved when the natural is sacrificed completely to the civilized.

From the beginning, Gelsomina's life with Zampanò is compartmentalized and based on role. The nature-civilization division of the first sequence becomes a split between personal and professional aspects of existence. The presence of each is evident in Gelsomina's function as both a companion ("wife") and a theatrical assistant and in Zampanò's use of the van as both home and workplace. An alternation between roadside (personal) activity and public performance suggests a relative balance at first. However, the balance proves more apparent than real. The first, and most extensive, roadside scene is given almost entirely to theatrical training, and Zampanò only turns to more "intimate" matters (forcing Gelsomina to

spend the night in the van) after she has succumbed to his brutal professional "education." Though Zampanò eventually seems to develop a sense
of appreciation for Gelsomina, it is the result not of genuine personal interaction (he refuses to answer any of her questions about himself or Rosa),
but of their success (largely through Gelsomina's performance in the "cun"
routine) as *artistes*. In fact, what he seems to value most about her—the
fact that she is "amusing"—is the very thing that has helped make them
professionally successful.

As Zampanò refuses to deal with Gelsomina in a truly personal way, she
is forced to rely on her professional identity for satisfaction. She experiences a series of contrasts between acceptance as an *artiste* and rejection
as a person. After enjoying tremendous crowd response to the "cun" routine, she is temporarily abandoned by Zampanò for a prostitute. (Even
this early in the film, the potential intimacy of the roadside has been left
behind for a crowded restaurant, and Zampanò has begun to deny Gelsomina even the role of sexual partner.) The following morning, when
Gelsomina cannot rouse the dead-to-the-world Zampanò and moves off in
despair, she rekindles her spirits by putting on a brief and well-received
comedy routine for a young girl. Most significant, after captivating a group
of children and entertaining the secluded Oswaldo at a wedding celebration, Gelsomina returns to Zampanò only to be crushed when he abandons her to have sex with Theresa.

The subordination of personal identity to artistic persona is particularly
clear from the way in which Gelsomina's powers of awareness awaken.
During the roadside training sequence, as Zampanò tries a variety of comedic hats on her, Gelsomina's face, eyes, and imagination come fully
alive. She responds with her own little dance, only to be quashed by Zampanò and forced to repeat the phrase "Zampanò is here" while she mechanically beats a drum. The fact that Gelsomina is awakened only by
costuming suggests her need—given the limitations of personal life—to
escape into make-believe. The fact that her attempt to unite make-believe
with her own natural expressiveness is thwarted by Zampanò suggests
that when she *does* escape into "art" and persona, it will be at the cost of
originality.

During the wedding sequence, Gelsomina's awakening consciousness
is again linked to costuming and her life as an *artiste*. She has two vivid
moments of awareness: her encounter with Oswaldo and her recognition
that Zampanò is going off to have sex with Theresa. Yet, in each case the
face that is illuminated by sudden understanding is that of a clown. For
the first sustained period in the film, Gelsomina is dressed wholly as a
performer and has abandoned her cape whose "wings" suggested her capacity for self-transcendence. She is now dressed in a long, masculine,
military overcoat. Moreover, both moments of awareness occur in the

very midst of playacting. She is in the process of entertaining Oswaldo when she has her epiphany of kinship and wonder, and she and Zampanò exchange highly theatrical winks of complicity (their moment of greatest—yet most artificial—rapport) just before Gelsomina realizes what is really going on.

Her experience with Oswaldo is particularly significant as an indication of what has happened by this point in the film. Like Gelsomina at the beginning, Oswaldo is a child; he is "not like the others," and he is mysterious, unfathomable in his "strangeness." However, while Gelsomina was willing and able to display her uniqueness at the very beginning, Oswaldo is reduced to mute withdrawal. And while Zampanò and his rudimentary world of civilization were willing at least to appropriate the qualities Gelsomina embodied, society now can view them only as an embarrassment or a spectacle. Oswaldo is hidden away, in the jealous custody of a nun, where the only people who visit him are children who are forced to view him largely as a freak.

(As the nun and the religious ritual of marriage suggest, Zampanò and Gelsomina are entering a world of institutions. Uniforms—military, religious, and social—abound here, and Zampanò uses sex with Theresa to acquire a pin-striped suit. In its emphasis on growing institutionalization, the wedding sequence serves as the threshold between agraria and the man-made world of the city. Succeeding sequences move to a large town and then to Rome.)

Through Oswaldo, Gelsomina encounters the very things which are being muted—or preserved only on the level of "art" or spectacle—in herself. Seeing herself in him, she experiences (her own) uniqueness only as abnormalcy, leading to isolation and fear. Self-consciousness becomes consciousness only of alienation. As a result, she is further inclined to suppress her originality and to deny true awareness by finding less demoralizing substitutes.

The Oswaldo sequence also highlights an emerging split between head and spirit, body and matter. Oswaldo's name means "the power of godliness." Gelsomina must ascend a flight of stairs to reach him; he is guarded by a religious representative, and Gelsomina's encounter with him is profound, numinous, awe-inspiring. At the same time, Zampanò is on ground level, gulping down food, talking with the self-assertively physical Theresa, and about to descend into the cellar to have sex. As Gelsomina's intelligence develops and as Zampanò continues to repress his own, they begin to live their lives on separate levels. In this instance—and indicative of what will recur throughout the film—she ends up back down on his, defeated by his unfeeling behavior.

Finally, in serving as a mirror or "projection" through which Gelsomina encounters herself, Oswaldo suggests that Gelsomina is becoming increasingly externalized—that her loss of identity has reached the point where she is about to begin living only through others. (The notion of "God" is introduced at this point as an abstraction and convention on which people begin to rely once they have lost their own godliness or capacity for self-transformation.)

Gelsomina's next moment of awakening—following Zampanò's adventure with Theresa—makes clear that she is, indeed, beginning to live largely through externals. Angered and depressed by Zampanò's infidelity, she is suddenly revived by the memory of a song she heard on the radio, and she asks Zampanò to teach her the trumpet. Her brightening of mood seems largely inspired by the light bulb she has been standing next to. The song and the radio are also external and, even more than the light bulb, can be seen as forms of surrogate consciousness. (They are "voices" that invade and take over the mind.) The song is particularly significant, for it will later be associated with *Il matto*, who clearly comes to function as Gelsomina's "borrowed" intelligence.

Gelsomina's sudden preoccupation with the song is a denial of her present situation. For the first time since she started communicating with Zampanò, she fails to confront him directly with her concerns about his behavior. Moreover, enlightenment, which was earlier equated with self-expression and creativity (her dance with the comedic hats), is now equated with escape.

This urge to escape, in turn, leads to a failed attempt to leave Zampanò—which is established largely in terms of the personal/professional division we discussed earlier. As she prepares to desert, Gelsomina announces: "I'm fed up. Not from the work. I like the work. I like being an *artiste*. It's *you* I don't like." Here she clearly sets things out in terms of alternatives: her work versus her personal relationship with Zampanò. Moreover, in stating a preference, she chooses her "career." This strongly suggests that her eventual return to him will offer no chance for a direct or personal relationship but will be based on Gelsomina's need for the life of an *artiste*.

By the time Gelsomina makes her temporary break with Zampanò, her identity and individuality have been eroded to the point that she has little initiative. As soon as she reaches a major thoroughfare, she runs out of energy and sits down by the side of the road. She must be fueled by the appearance of three musicians, dressed in military outfits, and lost in their own performance (they do not relate to Gelsomina at all). Once they appear, she is reduced to a follower. Moreover, she is led to a town filled with narrow streets and alleys (the "road" at its most restrictive), where a religious procession is in progress. Here she is pushed and pulled, directed and redirected, forced to go with the flow of the mob.

Throughout her journey, she is associated with images of crucifixion and martyrdom. And when she is confronted by the procession, Gelsomina does, in a sense, martyr herself—kneeling and adoring the images paraded in front of her.

Born out of this is *Il matto*. A heavenly apparition on his high wire, he is a "god" to be "worshipped." Known only by a stage name, he is pure role. First seen as a shadow on the side of a building, he is a projection more than a person. Dressed as an angel (a religious and theatrical "cliché") and born out of the religious, institutional, life of the town, he is strongly associated with tradition and convention. Finally, "crucified" on the cross formed by his tightrope and balancing pole, he is another image of martyrdom. He personifies, in short, everything to which Gelsomina is falling prey.

He also introduces a new phase in the film's analysis of the civilizing process. Whereas Zampanò introduced civilization at the point where it met and dominated nature, *Il matto* embodies it when nature and natural relatedness are replaced by illusion. Whereas Zampanò introduced rudimentary, practical intelligence, *Il matto* will promote idealization, fantasy, higher but *false* consciousness (the only kind that can emerge in a society that has lost touch with reality). His false consciousness, in turn, will become a form of "madness" as the meaning of his name—"the mad one"—suggests. (He is called "The Fool" in subtitled and dubbed prints, a name that is also indicative of his function in the film.)

In effect—and though Gelsomina does not realize it—*Il matto's* appearance provides a "solution" to her dilemma with Zampanò. She can compensate for living with him by projecting everything of value onto *Il matto*. The fact that her identity is about to become caught up in his is suggested moments before she is tracked down by Zampanò, when she is called *matta* (the feminine of *matto*) by a *vitellone* in a town square.

Once Gelsomina and Zampanò are reunited, the action moves to the outskirts of Rome. As always in Fellini's early work, Rome is associated with institutional illusion (cf. Parmesani's revue, the *White Sheik* comic strip, the Vatican, the matrimonial agency). However, the city itself is not the principal source of illusion during the Roman phase of the film. Rather, it is the Giraffa circus to which Gelsomina, Zampanò, and *Il matto* now belong. As the Giraffa sequences indicate, the circus institutionalizes personal and domestic life. People spend *all* their time on their "job site," and the life of family and extended family is dedicated not to personal relationships but to work, money, performance, make-believe. More than ever characters are defined by role rather than true identity. In addition, once the three characters join up, they sacrifice the freedom and mobility of earlier scenes for the shelter of "the big top," and they begin living under the restraint of authority: Colombaioni, the patriarchal head of the circus, and the police who apprehend Zampanò.

Gelsomina's life becomes even more restrictive and impersonal. She is treated solely as a theatrical assistant by Zampanò, not at all as a companion. She, in turn, no longer asks Zampanò about himself, only about *Il matto*. Moreover, though as a circus member she is defined more than ever as an *artiste*, she is given no freedom to express herself through art. Zampanò uses her only to beat the drum (there is no equivalent to the "cun" routine), and he prevents her from developing a new act with *Il matto*.

Faced with the continued failure of personal experience, Gelsomina relies more than ever on external sources of fulfillment. Living in a circus world of spectacle, she becomes a consummate spectator, looking outside herself in starry-eyed fascination with *Il matto*. In addition, the division between personal and professional that was initially situated within Gelsomina, becomes projected outward into a split between Zampanò and *Il matto*. (She relies on Zampanò for her domestic existence, while her professional or artistic excitement derives entirely from *Il matto*'s routines and music.) Zampanò, who has denied Gelsomina a *truly* personal relationship, now, in effect "symbolizes" what is missing—offering further indication of how falsified experience is becoming.

Because the split is outside Gelsomina, the possibility for synthesis no longer exists, only the possibility for balance. (*Il matto*, as an equilibrist, introduces the notion at the appropriate narrative moment.) Moreover, balance is ruled out as soon as the two men are brought together. (*Il matto*'s balancing act is never performed during the circus sequences.) Instead, Gelsomina must resort to alternation—taking turns being with each. Even alternation does not work as the relationship between the men leads to open conflict which can only be resolved by imposed peace at the hands of Colombaioni and, eventually, the police. Finally, peace can be sustained only by elimination and separation. The police take Zampanò off to jail, and Colombaioni kicks both men out of the circus—sending them in separate directions.

The conflict between *Il matto* and Zampanò comes to embody the split between head and body, spirit and matter, that emerged in the Oswaldo episode. While Gelsomina's bodily existence remains tied to Zampanò, her mind and imagination live through *Il matto*. (The first time she hears him playing the song from the radio, she moves over to the circus tent and places her chin on a rope strung across the entrance—"severing" her head from her body.)[5] In the circus environment of art, theatricality, and performance, the *Il matto*–Zampanò relationship also turns into allegory: the Angel versus the Beast. The two men are so lacking in personal identity, so easily manipulated by what is outside them, that they begin playing the

Il matto, *the object of everyone's gaze, becomes a source of higher but false consciousness as characters begin to look outside themselves during the circus scenes.*

role of each other's opposite. *Il matto* cannot be near Zampanò without calling him an animal and a beast; Zampanò cannot be near *Il matto* without becoming bestial. Though both initially embodied something of the other (Zampanò was a comedian as well as a strong man; *Il matto* a physical *artiste* as well as a musician and "angel"), each becomes completely one-sided.

Naturally inclined toward the angelic over the bestial, Gelsomina lives more and more through *Il matto*, and he ultimately becomes her surrogate identity. In keeping with this, he displays many of the characteristics she possessed earlier: childlikeness, humor, adventurousness, spontaneity, creativity, awareness, the capacity for transcendence. However, while she embodied all these as personal qualities, he merely symbolizes them through art and affectation. (As his irritatingly phony giggle suggests, he tends always to be playacting.)

As Gelsomina projects herself onto *Il matto*, selfhood disappears and is replaced by the mere illusion of identity and meaningful existence. The crucial moment in this process occurs when Zampanò is jailed and *Il matto* is momentarily given free rein to fill Gelsomina's head with his philosophy or rationale for life: everything, even the smallest stone, has a purpose, but only God knows how or why. Both his thesis and Gelsomina's whole-sale acceptance of it illuminate all the major problems that now exist within the film.

1. Characters have stopped thinking for themselves. *Il matto* confesses that his philosophy comes from books he has read, and a moment's analy-sis reveals that his "insight" is nothing more than the utterly conventional Christian doctrine of Divine Providence. (His philosophy is so common-place that for thirty years film critics have accepted it unquestioningly, even claiming that it is Fellini's "message" to his audience!) Moreover, Gelsomina adopts *Il matto's* words as the basis for her existence, ending once and for all the struggle to develop her own consciousness. The words themselves, of course, deny the value or possibility of individual aware-ness—asserting, as they do, that only God knows what is going on.

At this point, another stage in *La Strada's* analysis of the civilizing pro-cess begins. A world that has imposed artificial structure at the cost of natural connection and has substituted false consciousness for reality, reaches the dead end of consciousness. Intelligence starts to self-destruct, and regression toward a primitive, precivilized state begins. Here we re-call a crucial statement by Fellini quoted in our introduction: "There is a vertical line in spirituality that goes from the beast to the angel, and on which we oscillate. Every day, every minute carries the danger of losing ground, of falling down again toward the beast."[6]

2. All possibility for unity *within* experience is gone. "Purpose" in *Il matto's* scheme of things should equate with meaningful interrelationship between one person or thing and everything else. Since purpose and re-lationship are only provided and known by "God," however, there can no longer be any inherent meaning to experience. Even human authorities (Colombaioni and the police) have lost their ability to make order. All now hinges on an abstraction. (Fellini is not denying the truly religious notion of a divine power active in the world and in each of us. He is denying the validity of a God who is a mere Scholastic tool invented to compensate for the loss of personal meaning and initiative.)

3. Life, purpose, and love are reduced to bleak instrumentalism—a nat-ural outgrowth of the purchase of Gelsomina. *Il matto's* words are largely in response to Gelsomina's despairing remark: "I am no good to anyone." At first he tries to determine what skills she has (what she *is* "good for"). When she indicates that she does not have any, he resorts to his philoso-phy which is introduced wholly in terms of service and use: "I don't know what this stone is good for, but it must serve for something, because if it's useless, everything is useless. . . . Even you serve some purpose. . . ."

Reassured by his mechanistic view of things, Gelsomina uses *Il matto's* rhetorical question—"If you don't stay with him, who will?"—as her rationale for committing herself to Zampanò. This is the slimmest basis yet for their relationship. Moreover, by adopting "service" as the principal condition of their relationship, Gelsomina accepts the most traditional, the most unliberated, of female roles. (This, along with the fact that *Il matto's* philosophy is mere Christian doctrine, reveals how fully the characters have succumbed to traditional modes of experience by now.) In effect she commits herself to a life of self-denial and martyrdom.

4. The split between reality and illusion has become irremediable. The grim reality of Gelsomina's situation is suggested by her remark: "I am tired of living." It is explicit in the fact that Zampanò has regressed to murderous violence, threatening *Il matto* with a knife. Yet, instead of going off with the circus or with *Il matto* (she is offered both options), she makes the absurd decision to impose *Il matto's* philosophy on Zampanò. The extent to which she has become removed from reality is immediately suggested when she takes the stone given her by *Il matto* and begins staring foolishly at it. She shuts out everything around her, including him, as she invests the little rock with enormous symbolic import. Whereas she was earlier transfixed by a real figure with actual, visible talent (*Il matto* on his tightrope), she is now mesmerized only by abstraction.

The characters' forced abandonment of the circus following the fight between Zampanò and *Il matto* is a seeming return to reality from a world of artifice. However, the roles and illusions acquired in the circus environment make it impossible for the characters to reintegrate with the real world. (Indicatively, the road now confronts them with the most mundane of problems: Zampanò runs low on gas, the weather turns threatening, *Il matto* has car trouble.) Zampanò plays "the Beast" even more completely and assumes the new role of criminal which his night in jail has given him. He tries to steal silver hearts at a convent, he beats Gelsomina when she refuses to assist, then he beats up *Il matto* and becomes an unwitting murderer. Gelsomina ignores the reality of Zampanò's worsening behavior, as she clings to her symbolic pebble and *Il matto's* words. The dramatic change that has occurred since the beginning is highlighted by a brief scene in which she and Zampanò return to the sea. Though she rushes down to the water in initial excitement, she quickly turns away to pester Zampanò with her new fantasies about their relationship—and to renounce her real home ("now . . . my home is with you"). As the scene concludes she is moving farther and farther from the sea.

The denial of nature and reality is best exemplified by the convent sequence. Convent life is, in itself, a retreat from the world, and as an isolated, entirely female, community dedicated to "God," the convent in *La*

Strada proves to be even one step beyond the circus as an artificial "family" committed to illusion. Moreover, as a rather simple-minded nun who befriends Gelsomina says: "We change convents every year . . . so we don't get attached to worldly things. Like the place where we live. Or a plant even. Thereby forgetting the most important thing: God." These words, like *Il matto*'s, are commonplace Christian "wisdom," yet—particularly in the context of the film—they are life-denying and escapist. Paradoxically, they are also antispiritual, antireligious, for how can one live a morally responsible, loving existence by remaining "unattached"?

At the convent, Gelsomina is coaxed one step further into abstraction. The nun, believing that she is married, remarks: "You follow your husband, and I, Mine [i.e., God]." Acting on this notion, Gelsomina turns Zampanò into her god and actually broaches the subject of marriage: "Once I wanted to [die] rather than stay with you. But now I'd even marry you." This strengthening resolve to follow Zampanò, no matter what, is further evidence of Gelsomina's tendency toward self-sacrifice and martyrdom. Moreover, the nun's words enable her to justify that tendency in conventionally Christian terms by turning *Il matto*'s philosophy into a quasi-religious commitment. (Like *Il matto*, the nun is associated with crucifixion—standing, the last time we see her, in the shadow of an enormous cross.)

Gelsomina's willingness to embrace the institution of marriage is another sign that she, through *Il matto* and the nun, has succumbed to tradition and convention. (The point is made that the convent is 1,000 years old, and—intriguingly—the words *convento* and *convenzione* derive from precisely the same root.) More profoundly and tragically than ever in Fellini's work, marriage as an institution is seen as a substitute for meaningful union.

The withdrawal of Zampanò and Gelsomina into separate realms of criminality and pseudotheology is one of the many ways in which divisiveness continues to grow. A more obvious indication lies in the initial absence of *Il matto*. The "Angel" and the "Beast" can no longer live in the same world. The moment they come together, one is destroyed.

In the absence of *Il matto*, Gelsomina takes on the role of Angel. *She* begins to call Zampanò a beast and to imply sharp distinctions between mental activity and mere mindless, physical, existence: "you're a beast. You don't think." In so doing, she not only externalizes herself further (becoming *La matta*, as it were), she further erodes any chance for unification. Instead of trying to balance or alternate opposites through *Il matto* and Zampanò, remaining open to both options, she now becomes one half of the division herself. Consequently, despite her thoughts to the contrary, she is irrevocably alienated from Zampanò.

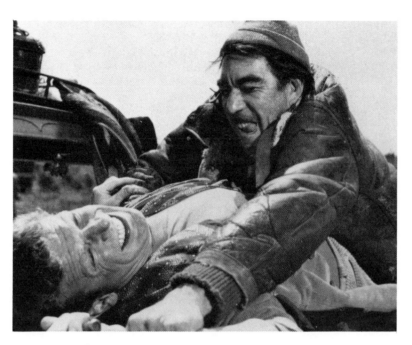

As life turns to allegory, the Beast destroys the Angel, and higher consciousness—even as an illusion—is eliminated.

By now, the division between Angel and Beast, mind and body, has become an outright divorce between ineffectual consciousness and brute physical necessity. Having lost all touch with reality, consciousness or thought can no longer influence it and, concomitantly, reality is now unredeemed by spirit or imagination. This is made clear when *Il matto*, the film's main source of consciousness, reappears and encounters Zampanò—the reality principle stripped of creative possibility. All *Il matto's* angelic powers are gone. Once a skywalker, he is now grounded. (His association with the earth, hence his surrender to the pull of gravity, is heavily emphasized.) Moreover, he is helpless in the grasp of Zampanò. Gelsomina, too (*Il matto's* angelic "stand in" during recent scenes), is helpless. She can only watch in paralyzed horror as *Il matto* is beaten and dies.

The killing of *Il matto* is the crucial event in the film's analysis of a false and self-destructive civilizing process. It marks the end of everything even remotely associated with higher consciousness. Not only is *Il matto* gone, but Gelsomina reacts to his death by surrendering all intelligence and withdrawing into a state of shock. That leaves Zampanò, who has explicitly repudiated conscious life—responding to Gelsomina's "you never think" with: "because there's nothing to think about. Go to sleep." Instead of true consciousness, we have instrumental reason: Zampanò's insistent pursuit of work and subsistence and his continuing need and use of Gelsomina for that end.

Gelsomina's madness reveals the extent to which she has sacrificed her identity. She has allowed *Il matto* to function so completely as her surrogate consciousness that when he dies, so does her own mind. His death, in effect, becomes hers.

Though Zampanò, by the time of *Il matto's* death, has been reduced almost entirely to brutish behavior, he has not sacrificed his humanity altogether. (In fact, his brutish acts to this point have been, paradoxically, quite human: an expression of frustration and rage as he feels his humanity increasingly compromised and repressed.) He can still feel an extraordinary sense of need for Gelsomina, becoming uncharacteristically solicitous as she falls ill and can no longer assist him. Moreover, Gelsomina serves as his conscience: her condition repeatedly reminds him of *Il matto's* death. Both his sense of need and his surrogate conscience link him, however tenuously, with a social universe. When he casts Gelsomina off, however, the links dissolve and there is nothing left to prevent Zampanò's final tragic deterioration.

His abandonment of Gelsomina marks a major event in the growing predominance of "absence" in the film. At the beginning, things such as consciousness, identity, and meaning were to a large extent present *within* Gelsomina and her world. However, through projection and abstraction, she became increasingly "absent" to herself—a process which culminated when she so thoroughly identified with the dead *Il matto*. Moreover, meaning came to depend not on immediate experience but on the remembered words of people absent (*Il matto's* philosophy, carried back onto the road by Gelsomina) and even more conclusively on a God who never manifests Himself. Finally, meaning itself disappeared with the death of *Il matto* and of conscious intelligence. Now that Gelsomina has been cast off, virtually everything in the film will be articulated in terms of absence, loss.

In the film's final phase, years after he has abandoned Gelsomina, Zampanò hears a young woman humming the song Gelsomina had inherited from *Il matto*. She is, for a moment, "reincarnated." However, the manner of her reincarnation only serves to emphasize that she is irrevocably gone. Moreover, she and everything she embodied are "dead on arrival" in the very act of reincarnation. (A poster advertising the American film *D.O.A.* is prominently displayed behind Zampanò as the woman recalls

In a world without Gelsomina or Il matto, *Zampanò is reduced to brutish futility, then to inertia, as* La Strada *comes to a close.*

Gelsomina.) Not only do we discover that Gelsomina has died, but she has no identity in the present. She is referred to only as a "girl" by the woman—and is not referred to at all by Zampanò. (The latter is a subtle indication of how repressed Zampanò's humanity is by now.) Furthermore, Zampanò is told that the local mayor could not determine who she was upon her death. Even Gelsomina's consciousness is dead in the retelling: "She never spoke. She seemed crazy. [*Matta* is used, linking her again with *Il matto*.] She never said anything, she just cried. One morning she just didn't wake up." Gelsomina has evaporated and been replaced by the young woman who, in hanging out laundry, is herself repeatedly disappearing behind sheets.

Like Gelsomina, Zampanò is largely dead on arrival. When we first see him, he is solitary, mechanical, and unfeeling as he rejects the company of a female performer and wolfs down most of an ice cream cone in one bite. He has apparently cast off his van, the emblem of his independence and openness to experience. He has made no attempt to replace Gelsomina, as he once replaced Rosa, to fulfill an urge for relatedness and love on some level. With the absence of his mobile home and female companionship, he is now definable solely in terms of work. (Unlike the Giraffa circus, the one he is now with shows no evidence of family or community.)

The story of Gelsomina offers him one last opportunity to awaken. Unfortunately, as his failure even to refer to her suggests, he is not up to it. He remains mute at the end of the woman's story and does not act on her suggestion that he find out more from the mayor. The next time we see him, he is performing his chain act in a state of complete numbness. (He fails to break the chain before we dissolve to the next scene.) Then, he represses awareness by getting violently drunk.

At this point, the final stage of regression occurs. Zampanò abrogates all social bonds by getting in a fight, hitting the one person who has identified himself as his friend and, most important, shouting "I don't need anyone. I just want to be alone." These final words make clear that Zampanò has jettisoned his one remaining tie to the human race: his sense of need.

He then stumbles in darkness and in a stupor beyond the town and circus, beyond all civilized structure, out to the sea. He returns not only to the origins of the film (without the crucial presence now of either Gelsomina or of light) but to the origins of evolution. He douses himself with water in a clumsy, drunken way that bespeaks the very impossibility of baptism or a sacramental relation to nature. He then stumbles back onto the shore and collapses to a sitting position. Looking tragically simian, he experiences one final burst of sentience as he looks to the heavens and confronts the outer image of his own vast emptiness. He can respond only with grunts of terror. Then he slumps forward, face down, turned away from the last bit of dim illumination offered by the night sky. He lies motionless, "dead" upon the beach. The fall back to the beast and beyond even that—to mere inanimate existence—is complete. Complete also is Fellini's apocalyptic vision of a fatally flawed civilizing process that bears the seeds of its own destruction and leads only to the ultimate denial of civilization and humanity.[7]

La Strada and Fellini's Imaginative Development

The importance of La Strada in Fellini's growth as an artist is, for the most part, self-evident. The film marks a major advance in complexity in terms of both characterization and narrative structure. The metaphoric richness, in turn, generates the "poetic" style for which the film was attacked by Marxists and praised by virtually everyone else. Without sacrificing the concreteness upon which aesthetic experience depends, Fellini abandons realism, verisimilitude, in order to articulate things more purely and directly in imaginative terms. Characters are not "people" first and embodiments of aesthetic significance second, nor are events "real" first and foremost. They are defined principally by what they embody on an imaginative level. They possess the concreteness of imaginative, spiritual experience rather than the concreteness of quotidian reality.

Because Fellini is able in La Strada to invest his characters with so much potential and complexity, he is able to create a world more fully human and—in its ultimate destruction—more fully tragic. The growing strength of his characters moves him yet closer to stories such as The Nights of Cabiria and 8½, in which potential and worth are realized rather than sacrificed.

In acknowledging the importance of La Strada, one must, of course, acknowledge the importance of Giulietta Masina (Gelsomina). As Fellini has remarked countless times, she has served as an indispensable source of vision. La Strada is the first of three Fellini films in which she has played the main character (The Nights of Cabiria and Juliet of the Spirits have been the other two). Each has been crucial to Fellini's development as an artist. "Giulietta is a special case. She is not just the main actress in a number of my films, but their inspiration as well. . . . So, in the case of Giulietta's films, she herself is the theme" (FF, 105).

7

Il Bidone

Il Bidone (The Swindle, 1955) is often considered the least successful of Fellini's early films. It was shot within two months and hastily prepared for presentation at the Venice Film Festival. As a result, it suffers from some minor flaws in editing and continuity. More problematic, it seems on first viewing to lack the resonance of *La Strada* and *I Vitelloni,* largely because of the inexpressive nature of its main character, Augusto. However, repeated viewings reveal a dignity and resourcefulness that make Augusto's tragic fate just as moving as that of Gelsomina and Zampanò, and close analysis reveals the film to be in many ways as interesting as *La Strada.*

Il Bidone introduces two elements to the Fellini canon: the mid-life crisis and "creative negation." Augusto is the first Fellini character to confront the fear of aging and dying without having lived a meaningful life. Though his efforts end in failure, his film-long purpose is to redeem his past and to create something of value in the present. "Creative negation" will be discussed in greater detail later. Briefly, it is the capacity on the part of both Augusto and Fellini to push tragedy to the point where it annuls itself, negating the negative as it were, and restoring the possibility of creative activity.

Il Bidone is divided into five "days." They are highly artificial in that the events within them often seem discontinuous and could well have taken place on separate days. However, they are unified by their chronological progression from morning to afternoon and, on three occasions, through night to dawn. Their artificial nature is consistent with the problem of contrivance throughout the film, and their discontinuity helps reinforce the lack of connection within the lives of characters.

Day One

The opening scene of *Il Bidone,* like that in *La Strada,* offers a relatively promising setting. However, the verdant countryside where the crooks meet is the only congenial setting in the film—and one from which the

Augusto, in his final moments of delirium, reaches out for community and salvation, only to encounter death.

characters remain largely detached. Their conference takes place on a stone bridge, their clerical garb makes them look out of place, and Picasso's appreciative remarks about the landscape go unacknowledged by the others. The characters' inauthenticity is evident from their disguises, and their lack of autonomy is clear in their reliance on "Boss" Vargas. Their relations are mediated by money, by a job, by roles, and by the common goal of cheating others. There is much less sense of possibility here than at the beginning of *La Strada*. There is no potentially creative figure such as Gelsomina. Picasso is the closest we get, but buried under a pseudonym and a priest's cassock, he is much closer to *Il matto* (playacting, false consciousness) than Gelsomina. The fact that Richard Basehart plays both Picasso and *Il matto* makes their similarity all the more striking.

Augusto is established from the start as the most withdrawn. He exemplifies his last name, Rocca ("fortress" as well as "rock"), concealing all emotion behind a hard and sullen exterior. Here, as throughout much of the film, the effort he makes to conceal his feelings is evidence of extraordinary inner struggle—and of a tragic insistence on suppressing personal experience.

Much as the brief opening scene offers the only appealing setting in *Il Bidone*, the first extended sequence—which takes place on a farm—offers the best example of a potentially integrated existence. As both home and workplace, the farm seems free of the division between personal and professional aspects of life that we saw early in *La Strada*. It allows for an organic, self-sustaining existence. However, there appears to be farm *ownership* but no *farming*: nothing seems to be growing. Moreover, a young girl and baby are expelled from the farmhouse as soon as the crooks arrive, leaving only two sisters whose advanced age further implies a world beyond fertility. The thieves then proceed to devalue the very nature of farming. Their method of swindling—burying fake treasure with a "corpse," digging both up, then selling the treasure to farm owners—is a travesty of planting and harvesting, and it makes the only crops grown in the film fake jewelry and old bones.

In setting up the fraud, Augusto pretends to produce a letter of confession and remorse, written at the point of death by a thief who killed his accomplice and buried him on the farm. Some stolen jewelry is supposedly buried with the corpse—jewelry that can be kept by the two sisters if they pay Augusto for 500 masses to be said for the salvation of the murderer's soul. As a story of death and betrayal among thieves, Augusto's tale serves as prophecy: he will later try to swindle his accomplices and end up being killed by them. (The controlling power of prophecy comes to characterize a world of tragic determinism as Augusto sacrifices his freedom.) As a quest for atonement and salvation, the letter introduces renewal and redemption as major themes. It also suggests an inherent falseness to the way in which both are sought. Not only is the letter itself a lie, but one cannot "buy" salvation—or gain it through having priests say masses for one's soul. Spiritual attainment (as always in Fellini's films) is either self-created or it is an illusion.

The impossibility of atonement is further suggested by the fact that one can never truly compensate for murder: the victim cannot be brought back to life. (In addition to being a parody of farming, the swindle, in its burial and disinterment of a "corpse," becomes a parody of death and resurrection.)

The farm fraud, of course, has strong political and socioeconomic overtones. The thieves' impersonation of religious figures is only plausible because the church *has* become materialistic and *does* expect payment for its religious services. At the same time, the victims are caught up in the capitalist game; otherwise they would not be easily fooled and so accepting of the premise that money can buy atonement.

The use of religion merely as a moneymaking front points to the most profound problem of all in *Il Bidone:* the substitution of materialist values for spiritual goals. Augusto is particularly at fault. Instead of responding to his midlife crisis by undergoing spiritual and moral development, he tends only to seek out monetary schemes of self-improvement.

The swindle introduces "exile" as a major problem in the film. Not only are the young girl and child expelled from the farmhouse, so are the two sisters, as they must go off in search of money for the Masses. When they return, they never reenter the house. They stand and wave gratefully to their exploiters—dispossessed not only of money but (figuratively) of home. In a world where characters repeatedly sell themselves out, everything tends to end up on the outside. Moreover, the division between inside and outside comes to reflect the division between personal and professional aspects of life. In fact, in a film where physical and material reality replaces spiritual value, vacancy on the inside comes to represent the absence of spirit and self within.

The night sequences following the swindle reveal that the characters live lives neatly (and quite conventionally) divided between work and leisure, public and private. In addition, they even divide into private and public among themselves. Picasso goes home to his family, while Roberto escorts Augusto to a nightclub. (Picasso and Roberto externalize for Augusto his conflict between personal and professional, much as Zampanò and *Il matto* did for Gelsomina.)

The night sequences illustrate not only this division but the inadequacy of everything private. Picasso never really gets home; he only gets as far as the staircase to his apartment and insists that Iris and Silvana join him outside. Since this is the closest he ever gets to home, and since neither

Augusto nor Roberto is shown to have one, home is never a reality for the main characters in the film.

Once Picasso and Iris are reunited, gifts quickly replace direct contact, and the discussion of money, debts, and Picasso's ambitions as a painter replaces truly personal matters. As this occurs, Silvana is treated more and more like an object. She is picked up, carried around, and put down, but never really treated as a human being. By the sequence's end, Picasso and family, like the two farm sisters, are "exiled": moving down a public thoroughfare, away from the camera eye and, by implication, away from whatever home they once shared.

At the same time, the nightclub attended by Roberto and Augusto is a haven for homeless or displaced persons. The waiters and musicians are Italian, but there is a black (American) entertainer, an English dancing girl, and American tourists. In addition, Roberto orders French champagne while the entertainer provides an absurd, Felliniesque image of rootlessness: dancing on roller skates!

Here Augusto commits himself to the first in a series of false attempts at renewal, drunkenly claiming: "I'm going to go back to working alone" (*TS*, 164). As an assertion of independence, it is immediately undercut by his reliance for company on the English dancing girl. As an equation of independence with isolation, it recalls Zampanò's words at the end of *La Strada* and points to the radical alienation Augusto will experience by the end of the film, when he does try to "work alone" by turning on his partners.

This sequence, too, ends in exile as Roberto, Augusto, and their companions leave the nightclub at dawn and move away from the camera eye, down a deserted street.

Days Two and Three

During the second and third days, personal life becomes so devalued that it can only survive as illusion by day four.

When Augusto masquerades as a government official, allotting new apartments to slum dwellers in exchange for a down payment, home and family are further eroded. Unlike the farm sisters, the slum tenants are so dissatisfied with their living conditions that they are, in effect, rootless. Their reliance on government suggests how institutionalized the home has become. (Government is implicated here, as the church was earlier, as a materialist institution.) Moreover, obsession with housing is such that the family proper is of secondary importance, as is poignantly implied by the repeated image of a child unattended on a rooftop.

This time Picasso never gets home following the swindle. Moreover, Silvana never appears. (She is reduced to a few nostalgic references by

Picasso to *la bambina.*) Iris, in turn, gets dragged into the world of Augusto's old Mafioso friend Rinaldo, who has exiled *his* family to Switzerland. Following Rinaldo's party, she and Picasso get into a heated argument, and the last time we see them together they are standing at right angles to each other, unreconciled.[1]

By the end of the third day not only have Iris and Silvana disappeared, but Picasso, reacting to his alienation, has gotten drunk. Feeling and emotion degenerate into mere ineffectual sentiment as Picasso can do nothing but bemoan the failure of his home life. Family (like meaning, consciousness, and identity in *La Strada*) becomes defined solely in terms of absence. Home, in a most profound way, is reduced to homesickness. The last time we see Picasso, he is standing alone, looking helplessly about him, and making no effort to carry out his expressed intentions of returning to Iris and Silvana. Since he never reappears, his separation from home and family is final, absolute.

Augusto himself explicitly contributes to the denial of family during his attempts to counsel Picasso. Unable to offer anything but negative commentary on Picasso's situation, he says: "In our kind of work you can't have a family. A man's got to be free. . . . You have to be a loner" (*TS*, 218).

Augusto continues to have no personal life other than through his relationship with Picasso. Moreover, his identity weakens as he becomes more dependent on others. He makes one brief attempt to fulfill his promise of working alone, but it is an instant failure as his mark turns out to be an older and wiser crook. He is then forced back on the authority of Vargas for the housing fraud. When he tries to revitalize his career through Rinaldo, he becomes little more than a supplicant—following his old friend around and entreating him to take him on as anything from a partner to a secretary. His entreaties get him nowhere, and by the third day he is completely dependent on Roberto, who sets up the overcoat fraud and provides both coats and car. His reliance is made all the more compromising by the fact that in the scene immediately preceding (after Roberto tried to steal a woman's compact at Rinaldo's) Augusto expressed utter contempt for Roberto: "If your mother wasn't worse than you she'd have strangled you when you were born" (*TS*, 199).

The disappearance of family life for Picasso, Augusto's explicit renunciation of family, and his increasing inability to act for himself all create the context in which Patrizia, Augusto's daughter, is introduced. Instead of making genuine personal experience possible for Augusto, she is (unwittingly) used by him merely to compensate for his lack of personal, family life. This lack is underscored when Patrizia's appearance comes as a surprise—in fact, a shock—not only to Augusto but to us. We discover that he has had a family throughout the film, which he has chosen to ignore until it was thrust upon him.

His alienation from his family is further emphasized when he fails to recognize Patrizia (she has to call out to him) and when it is revealed that he has not seen her in two years. She is presented entirely as an *outside* force (an apparition), and Augusto will become dependent on her just as he has been on Vargas, Rinaldo, then Roberto. He will try to redeem himself through her in a way that, though quite touching, is doomed to failure.

As Patrizia's role might suggest, there is a growing association of renewal and regeneration with empty symbolism. Rinaldo's party—a brawling celebration of the New Year—establishes this early on. (Significantly, Rinaldo's "toast" to the New Year has nothing of renewal in it: "It's midnight. Everything that's no good any more gets thrown out" [*TS*, 192].) However, it is most tragically suggested through Picasso. At one point in his drunken state, having collapsed to a sitting position, he rises with Augusto's assistance and his moment of recovery is associated with the sound of a baby's cry—to which neither he nor Augusto responds. Moments later, he is "baptized" by a few drops of falling rain. However, like Zampanò's trudge into the water at the end of *La Strada*, these signs of regeneration remain purely external. There is no spirit within to give them meaning. Picasso's continued sense of devastation after the rain makes clear that no redemption has taken place.

Again, images of exile abound. The second day ends with Roberto, having exited from Rinaldo's, moving off down the street to catch a cab; with Picasso and Iris stranded and estranged on the sidewalk; and with Augusto, having declined offers of company from Picasso and two prostitutes, walking alone at dawn, in the opposite direction of two revellers. Nearly all of day three takes place in exile—not only outdoors but outside Rome—culminating in the group's nighttime discussions in a deserted town. The final shot is of the bewildered and utterly dispossessed Picasso.

Day Four

The Patrizia-Augusto relationship, which takes up the whole of day four, is created through a couple of subtle narrative substitutions. The day is introduced by a dissolve from Picasso, looking all around him, to Patrizia doing much the same as she emerges through the gate of a church. At the same time, a verbal parallel is drawn between the prostitute telling Roberto and Augusto that she must be home at midnight and Patrizia telling Augusto she must be home by seven. Patrizia, in fact, becomes Picasso's replacement as an external locus of personal value for Augusto. Simultaneously, she comes to function figuratively as a prostitute—a woman whom Augusto tries to "buy" by volunteering to underwrite à bond she must post to finance her education. (Their relationship is mediated repeatedly by money. Augusto buys her a flower as soon as they meet—then buys her lunch, a movie, and ice cream before offering to pay for the bond.)

Patrizia clearly externalizes a number of positive values: home, family, femininity, youth, beauty, affection, innocence, love. Yet she is the most rootless—and ultimately the most compromised—female thus far. Unlike Picasso, she is never *shown* to have a home and family. Her mother (Augusto's wife) never appears, and Patrizia herself always begins and ends her appearances in the streets of Rome. Much like *Il matto*, she is a *symbol* rather than an *embodiment* of the things with which she is linked.

Equally important, Patrizia is thoroughly "institutionalized." The first time that she is introduced, she has just come from school. The second time, she has just come from church. Her goals are to become further institutionalized: to post a bond in order to become a cashier in order to go to teacher's college in order to be a teacher.

The limitations of her relationship with Augusto are most fully clarified during their two sustained conversations. First of all, during lunch, they both make an effort to initiate personal discussion. Augusto talks of his age, she talks of her mother. However, neither is able to respond appropriately to the other's remarks. Augusto, especially, evades the topic of his wife and, shortly thereafter, decides to retreat behind his dark glasses. As he takes them out, a cheap watch he tried to pawn off earlier appears and catches Patrizia's eye. It dominates the conversation, replacing all attempts at more intimate dialogue, and Augusto offers it to her as a gift. In effect, the watch becomes the basis of their relationship—implying (given its earlier use) that the relationship itself is a "swindle" or deception.

Second, at the movie theater, their conversation becomes part of an absurd "love scene" whose illusory nature is emphasized by the context. Augusto claims that the usherette thinks they are engaged. (Not only is there no evidence of this, but the very idea is both absurd and a bit perverse.) Then he plays the role of the possessive lover, asking her to keep her Sundays open for him. After this, their "love" is "sealed with a kiss" as she responds effusively to his willingness to pay the bond. The kiss coincides with the romantic, happy-ending music of the film that is just concluding. As though this were not enough to emphasize the illusoriness of it all, music from *The White Sheik*—Fellini's most satiric view of deluded "lovers"—begins to play!

Augusto, in his inauthentic quests for redemption, has lost touch with reality and become completely self-deceived. At this point, the film's title suggests not so much a world in which people fool or cheat one another, but a world in which they fool themselves.

Unfortunately for Augusto, reality quickly and violently reasserts itself as the brother of an old mark spots him and has him arrested. Despite all the seeming promise of day four, it too ends with exile. Augusto is marched off to the police station, and his concluding words to Patrizia—a harsh "Go home"—exile her forever from his life.

Day Five

On day five, with Picasso and Patrizia—Augusto's two surrogates or symbols for personal life—removed, he goes back to work. Having become temporarily expansive in the company of Patrizia, he now withdraws more than ever into his "fortress" of self-protection. To the extent that anything even illusorily personal remains, it is muted, repressed—notable, like Gelsomina in the final scenes of *La Strada*, only in its absence. This is most significantly reflected in the fact that we cannot determine *motive* for Augusto's actions leading up to his death. (We can hypothesize that he is moved by the desire to pay Patricia's bond, but there is no compelling evidence. In fact, dialogue which implied such motive in the screenplay has been eliminated from the film in an apparent attempt by Fellini to cloud the issue as much as possible.)[2]

The day begins with Augusto's release from jail—another instance of potential renewal. Yet renewal is now defined in largely negative terms: *not* being in prison. It is also defined in terms of repetition rather than advance, as Augusto goes back to Vargas and duplicates the farm fraud that opened the film. Finally, renewal is equated with callous exploitation of *everyone*. The one bit of novelty introduced is Augusto's attempt to swindle his accomplices as well as the farm family.

The death of home and family is again evident—this time through the lack of relationship among the fraud victims. The father gets swindled indoors while the mother waits outside. Susanna (the crippled daughter who, in her naiveté, recalls the nun in *La Strada*) lives in a world of her own both spatially and mentally. The sister, who (reportedly) works in the fields, never appears. The one moment of family contact—when the mother brings Augusto to Susanna—ends when Susanna tells her mother: "Go away." Equally important, the family suffers from the kind of instrumentalism that became so pervasive near the end of *La Strada*, as the members evaluate one another in terms of usefulness. Susanna is praised because of her skill at accounting ("she can calculate better than a teacher" [*TS*, 239]) and because of her embroidery. Her sister is discussed in terms of the amount of difficult labor she does.

The most significant event at the farm is not the swindle itself but Augusto's encounter with Susanna. Fellini's characterization of her is twofold and requires a twofold response. As a victim of infantile paralysis she is tragic and evokes our sympathy. At the same time, she traffics and even revels in her victimization. She creates a persona for herself—"the blissful martyr"—which she never wants to grow beyond. When Augusto raises the possibility that she might recover, not only does she say "It's impossible" (*TS*, 240), but she responds with amazement, fear, and dismay. Though she claims to believe in miracles, it is clear that the one miracle she could not tolerate would be a cure. In short, her affliction proves more emotional and moral than physical; she remains sadly "infantile"—fixated at age nine, when she contracted the disease.

Although she initially seems to display strength and courage in her role, her underlying weakness and fear become clear from her desperate reverence for Augusto, and from her agonized entreaties as he pulls away from her tight grasp: "Don't go away. . . . Pray for me!" (*TS*, 240).

One might expect Susanna to replace Patrizia as someone for whom Augusto can provide parental support and thus derive a sense of validation. (Susanna does, of course, replace Patrizia narratively, as Patrizia replaced Picasso.) However, Susanna's limitations and Augusto's own depressed moral state are such that she elicits not support but nihilism: "Our life . . . the life of so many people I know has nothing beautiful in it. . . . I have nothing to give you" (*TS*, 240).

It is within this context that Augusto's final swindle occurs. To a large extent, it is the enactment, the "fulfillment" of his nihilism. In stealing both from Susanna and from his friends he is asserting the meaninglessness of community, morality, and love. Moreover, in the course of the swindle he is forced to call upon Patrizia and use *her* merely as a means to an end. This becomes clear when his remark "I have a daughter [too]" (*TS*, 244) proves only a ploy to persuade the others that he has returned the money to Susanna's family. (He uses his "conscience" in precisely the same way when he disarmingly asks his companions: "Can't I have a conscience too?" [*TS*, 244].)

Augusto's attempted theft is also nihilistic in the sense that it cannot possibly work. Even if he were stealing for Patrizia, her earlier horrified response to the discovery that he was a crook has made it clear that she would never accept money from him. More immediately, the viciousness of his associates and his own history of deceit ensure that he will not be believed. In effect, then, his attempted swindle is suicidal—a kind of empty "martyrdom" in response to the futility of his life.

Augusto's movement toward death is presented in terms of yet another meaningless renewal or enlightenment, an ascent lacking in any spiritual significance, a final and tragically ironic "salvation." After being stoned and losing consciousness at night, Augusto is "reborn" to "see the light" at dawn. Not only does he awaken, he struggles from well down the hill all the way to the top, where he calls out to a group of passing women and

Spiritually paralyzed in his masquerade as a priest, Augusto is about to reject the clinging Susanna's pleas for company and comfort. Courtesy: Museum of Modern Art/Film Stills Archive.

children. As delirious and oblivious to reality as Gelsomina was after *Il matto*'s death, he insists "I'm coming with you" (*TS*, 252), and his words are accompanied by a smile of satisfaction which (as the screenplay indicates) is the smile of salvation attained. At this moment, unnoticed by the women and children, he dies.

Unfortunately for Augusto, his death *is* his salvation; the only solution to a life which is no longer worth living. It is also his ultimate exile. Alone on a barren, stony cliff, he is excluded once and for all from human community, as well as from the community of the living. He ends the film as just another rock (*rocca*) on the hillside, reduced even more emphatically than Zampanò to mere inanimate existence.

Il Bidone and Fellini's Imaginative Development

Though *Il Bidone* has not been as well received as other Fellini films, few of his movies have been more important in his growth as an artist. It is reasonably safe to say that without *Il Bidone* there could not have been *The Nights of Cabiria*—and without *Cabiria* there could not have been the extraordinary films of individuation from 8½ through *Roma*.

For the first time, Fellini envisions a world that exists beyond the tragedy of the main characters. And for the first time, Fellini's camera eye is able to free itself from its tale of alienation and move toward images of wholeness. As Augusto brings about his own destruction, he takes with him all the limitations with which he has been associated and paves the way for a "miracle"—a moment of genuine renewal and salvation—to emerge within the narrative. The women and children who appear so unexpectedly are the opposite of everything Augusto has become. They are a model of community, harmony, self-expression, motion, and spontaneity; they "marry" man and nature, male and female, the human and the man-made, adult and child. Their miraculous appearance signals the rebirth of possible wholeness. They are the seed out of which grows *The Nights of Cabiria*: a film in which the main character will follow Augusto's trail to the brink of desolation but will achieve reintegration—appropriately among a community similar to that at the end of *Il Bidone*.

With *Il Bidone*, Fellini seems to have discovered that even tragedy is an expression of life's creative urges: life's way of killing off what gets in the way of creation. In this context Augusto presents himself as a major advance in Fellini's vision. He is the first Fellini character who is an agent of the life process, as well as its victim. In his own way he functions as a creator—an artist of alienation who turns his own destructive powers on himself to cancel them out. He negates the negative, makes way for the positive, and martyrs himself (unwittingly) in the name of greater life. In this respect, he is precursor to Marcello in *La Dolce Vita*, who, in a more profound and apocalyptic way, will take negation as his principal mode of activity and perform a creative function—if not for himself, at least within the world of his film.

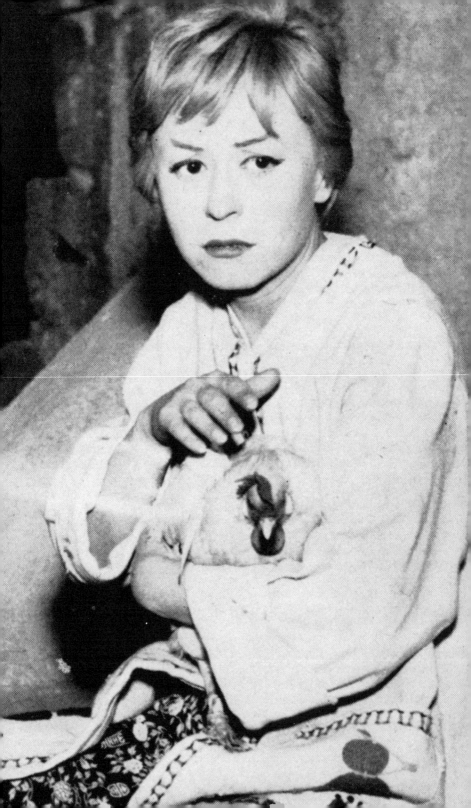

8

The Nights of Cabiria

Because *Il Bidone* was not well received, Fellini found it difficult to find backing for another film. He had to deal with eleven producers in the process of getting *The Nights of Cabiria* (1956) made.[1] The struggle to finance *Cabiria* was well worth it, however. The film was immensely successful, not only in Europe but in America, where it brought Fellini his second Oscar. The impact of *Cabiria*—as with his first Oscar-winning film, *La Strada*—was largely the result of a marvelous performance by Giulietta Masina. In range and subtlety her Cabiria is an even more impressive portrayal than was her Gelsomina.

The character Cabiria has precedents by way of both her name and Giulietta. Not only did Masina play the prostitute Cabiria in *The White Sheik*, but another Cabiria lent her name to an extraordinarily successful Italian silent film (1913). While Fellini's two Cabirias have much in common with each other, they differ sharply from the silent film character. Even though the film bears her name, the silent Cabiria is a minor and passive figure perpetually saved and ruled by external forces, particularly men. The nature of her captivity tends to change, but she is no more liberated at the end when she "finally . . . finds peace in the sincere love of a Roman patrician"[2] than she was earlier in the hands of pirates and the enemies of Rome. She proves to be little more than a stereotypical movie heroine, a mere projection of male fantasies with no life of her own: a "prostitute" in her own way. It seems that in naming his heroine after the silent screen figure, Fellini was out to redeem the original Cabiria—and the image of women in movies—from this subtle form of cultural prostitution.

Cabiria also serves to redeem Gelsomina. The connection between the two is present not only through Masina but through several subtle yet unmistakable allusions to *La Strada* in *The Nights of Cabiria*. At the first crucial moment of growth for Cabiria (when she faces the fact that her lover Giorgio has tried to kill her) she casts him off symbolically by burning all his belongings. Both her words and actions recall a moment of rebellion in *La Strada* when Gelsomina tells *Il matto* that she is going to burn all Zampanò's things and get free of him. In Gelsomina's case it is all

Cabiria ponders the question "What if I'd died?" after her near drowning at the hands of Giorgio.

69

talk; in Cabiria's, it is evidence that, from the beginning, she has a power of self-liberation that is lacking to Gelsomina. Moreover, once she has committed Giorgio's memory to flame, she arrives at her "workplace" (the Passeggiata Archeologica) in a motorcycle cart, driven by a male and reminiscent of Zampanò's van. However, it is much lighter and far more open than the van and, even more important, once Cabiria descends from it, she never relies on it again. Finally, as she packs to go off with Oscar, Cabiria makes a point of leaving behind a statuette of an owl—an image closely associated with Zampanò in *La Strada*.

Because *The Nights of Cabiria* is redemptive rather than tragic, it is a radical departure from Fellini's preceding films. Nonetheless, it incorporates many of the problems dealt with earlier in his career, largely through the leitmotiv of prostitution. Prostitution not only characterizes a world in which the feminine, loving, and personal are reduced to sexual commodity in a male-dominant society, but it functions figuratively to signify the willingness of characters to sell themselves out to illusions such as the bourgeois ideal of financial security, salvation through institutionalized religion, happiness ever after in marriage, and so on. Consequently, Cabiria's ability to abandon her life of prostitution becomes her ability also to free herself from her many self-protective and escapist fantasies.

Above all else, *The Nights of Cabiria* is a profoundly religious film.[3] It culminates a subtle progression in Fellini's early work toward an intensely personal revaluation of traditional religious concepts. Whereas a film such as *The White Sheik* treated the church as an institutional authority with little or no theological or spiritual substance, *La Strada* began to address notions such as Divine Providence, renunciation of the world, "marriage to God," and martyrdom. *Il Bidone*, in turn, was conceived largely in terms of redemption, death and rebirth, martyrdom, and salvation. In both these films, the theological dimension proved unredemptive. However, while theology itself was seen to be a problem in *La Strada* (belief in Divine Providence and in worldly renunciation impeded consciousness and growth), in *Il Bidone* the problem lay more with the characters. Augusto was "swindled" not because he sought to redeem his life, but because he repeatedly chose false means to that end.

In *The Nights of Cabiria*, Fellini takes the religious patterns he employed in *Il Bidone*, combines them with a creative main character, and tells a story of genuine death and resurrection, redemption, "salvation." In so doing, he does not become conventionally Catholic. Instead, he resurrects Christian doctrine from its institutional and repressive context, liberating what is truly religious and spiritual within it. Instead of affirming the authority of any church, *The Nights of Cabiria* affirms the validity of individual religious experience, the power of *self*-creation and re-creation.

At the same time, while *Cabiria* seems to work with traditional Christian distinctions between physical and spiritual life, body and mind, it does not do so in a conventionally dualistic way. Bodily existence is not an evil that must be renounced in favor of pure otherworldliness, but rather the necessary starting point for a process of moral and spiritual evolution. Though there tends to be a dualistic phase in the process, when Cabiria first discovers her intellectual and spiritual powers and perceives life in terms of division, experience is always *evolving from* matter to spirit, *transforming* matter *into* spirit. Fellini dynamizes, "temporalizes," and unifies concepts that remain static, spatial, and juxtaposed in Christian doctrine.

Finally, Fellini redeems traditional Christian notions of transcendence, innocence, salvation—all of which normally imply an escape from or denial of experience. Transcendence (as the suffix *trans* would suggest) is radical change *through* (not away from) experience—always associated with processes of *trans*-formation. Innocence is a fully open response to new experience as the result of having unified oneself through prior experience. Salvation is an illusion that Cabiria uses to push herself ever forward in the quest for a better life. It is never a final state of attainment that eliminates the responsibility for continued struggle and development. In the final moments of her story, Cabiria is back on the road, en route to more spiritual encounters, more challenges to make life and self anew.

In the opening moments of the film, Cabiria is little more than a body, seen from such a distance that she has virtually no individuality. When Giorgio steals her purse and shoves her into the Tiber, her near drowning and rescue (also shot from a distance) are principally physical events—and her "virtues" (energy, endurance, resiliency) are likewise physical. However, there is more than a hint here of baptism, death and resurrection, incipient spiritualization. More precisely, Cabiria's physical "rebirth" or resuscitation marks the birth of individuality, independence, and intelligence. When she comes to, her face is clearly revealed for the first time, a passerby identifies her as "Cabiria," she rebels against her rescuers, and she begins to wonder about Giorgio's whereabouts.

Her awakened mental powers lead Cabiria to her first major moment of personal development. After trying to ignore the fact that Giorgio has tried to rob and kill her, she begins to use her friend Wanda as a sounding board, relentlessly asking questions about Giorgio's motives. These questions lead her not only to acknowledge the truth about him but also to ask: "What if I'd died"[4]—marking the awakening of self-consciousness.

Cabiria's self-consciousness expresses itself in largely physical terms, as she uses her body to create poses and strike attitudes to impress the world. Seeing herself as a body, she sees herself as separate from everyone else. The words "Notice the difference between you and me," shouted by Matilde as Cabiria arrives at the Passeggiata, capture her own sense of separation. Her accompanying defensiveness and alienation manifest themselves when she immediately gets into a fight with Matilde.

The symptoms of emerging self-consciousness are not all so limited. In responding to her alienation, Cabiria senses something missing, as well as the need for change. Not only does she temporarily abandon the Passeggiata in a comic and futile attempt to compete with the more sophisticated hookers of the Via Veneto, she experiences the awakening of idealization, wonder, and rudimentary love through her encounter with the movie star Alberto Lazzari.

As his name suggests, Lazzari is a resurrective figure. His occupation is one of repeated death and rebirth, as he moves from one character and movie to the next. His career also endows him with the immortality that resurrection entails, since his celluloid images will long outlive his body. He is not only resurrective, he is resurrectable. In the course of his appearance, he is virtually brought back to life by Cabiria (the first time she significantly affects her world), as her company dissolves his surly self-centeredness and makes possible his reconciliation with Jessy.

With the appearance of Lazzari, death and resurrection evolve beyond mere physical events which Cabiria passively experiences. They become something which, like the movies, can be envisioned, made to happen. Self-transcendence and self-creation become imaginative possibilities. More specifically Cabiria, through Lazzari, refines four different ways of getting beyond herself: role-playing, vision, projection, and make-believe (all of which are, obviously, associated with movies).

Role-playing.   A role-player by profession, Lazzari appears at a point when Cabiria has taken to play-acting herself, affecting a "cool" exterior at the Passeggiata, trying to pass as a high-priced hooker at the Via Veneto, adopting a stubbornly self-assured pose for a nightclub doorman moments before Lazzari emerges. In response to the sensed limitations of her given identity, Cabiria is trying to improve upon it, and Lazzari helps things along by "casting" Cabiria in the role of replacement or "understudy" for Jessy. She adapts admirably, becoming a suitable and refreshing companion for Lazzari.

Vision.   When Cabiria is transported by Lazzari's appearance, it is his image that astounds her and her eyes that reflect her wonder. Moreover, consistent with his work in movies, Lazzari lives in a highly visual world—from his stagy fight with Jessy (played before the "audience" of Cabiria and the doorman), to the nightclub where he takes Cabiria, to the multimirrored, glassed, and imaged world of his villa. Within this context Cabiria learns to relate to the given—and particularly Lazzari—as image rather than matter. She settles for Lazzari's photograph instead of his body when Jessy reappears, and she ends her evening watching the reconciliation of Jessy and Lazzari through the bathroom keyhole. A room normally reserved for bodily functions becomes a "screening room" and Cabiria turns their relationship into a "film"—as is made clear by the concluding iris shot of the two lovers.

Projection.   When Cabiria is transported by Lazzari's appearance, it is clear that she is projecting onto him her dreams of romantic fulfillment—then worshipping him as the illusory object of her dreams. Narcissistic as this may be, it still marks the beginning of Cabiria's capacity for something other than mere physical love or prostitution.

Make-believe.   Like the movies he stars in, Lazzari traffics not just in images but in fantasy. Though he is surrounded by visual objects, he is also ruled by things unseen, whose presence is wholly mental. He refers to people absent (his maid) or who no longer exist (Beethoven), and his entire evening with Cabiria is predicated on the fact that Jessy is *not* there. Cabiria, too, begins to relate to things not present: asking Lazzari if he has any fish, talking passionately of her home, and describing in detail a scene from a movie. Ultimately, she outdoes Lazzari. Whereas he remains tied to things which, though absent, either were or are real, Cabiria moves to hypothesis: predicting that her friends will never "believe" (a word that will take on immense importance in succeeding scenes) that she spent the evening with him. She gravitates, in short, closer to the realm of the nonexistent and the merely possible.

This becomes even clearer the following morning. For one thing she leaves behind Lazzari's photo when she leaves his villa. For another, when she awakens ("reborn" again) in his bathroom, she gazes out the window and off into the distance—not back into the bedroom. For the first time, she looks *beyond* rather than *at* her world. No longer in the service of a given, visual environment, her eyes reflect a longing to penetrate the realm of the invisible. This gets her into immediate trouble. As she is trying to find her way out of the villa, she focuses so intensely on the distance that instead of seeing a glass door, she sees through it, and is rewarded with a stunning smack on the head. (The awakening of her head, to which the entire Lazzari sequence has conspired, is here "confirmed"—sacramentally and otherwise!)

Appropriately, the next major event in Cabiria's development is religious. Her readiness for it is established in a brief scene at the Passeggiata. While she and her friends debate whether or not they will attend a pilgrimage to the shrine of Divino Amore, a small procession appears. Cabiria again displays the capacity for wonder that was awakened by Lazzari, but here, as at the end of the preceding sequence, her attention is directed beyond her immediate world. As the pilgrims move through the

Passeggiata and down the road, they take Cabiria's eyes with them, far into the distance—in effect, to the "vanishing point."

When Cabiria arrives at the pilgrimage, she is wearing a bright white raincoat, which indicates her unconscious urge for enlightenment and reveals a growing capacity on her part to symbolize her inner feelings. The theme of the pilgrimage—Divine Love—takes Cabiria beyond the mere romantic attachment embodied by Lazzari. It offers her a model of love freed from sexuality and dependence (from prostitution). Through her absorption in the religious excitement, Cabiria acquires the incentive for transformation implicit in such love. She begs the Madonna, "Help me change my life," and following the religious services, she bemoans the fact that she and her friends have not been changed. Her prayers and complaints—as well as her assertion "I'll sell my house and everything . . . I'm going away"—make clear that she *has* changed dramatically, and has taken a crucial step toward spiritual death and rebirth.

Consistent with our earlier remarks about traditional Christian thought, the pilgrimage is given entirely to renunciation of the body—thus introducing the "dualistic phase" of Cabiria's growth. The events progress from bustling activity at the bottom of a hill to ascent and purely spiritual activity at the top. The ascent itself is given largely to mortification of the flesh, as many of the pilgrims inch their way forward on their knees, reciting the Stations of the Cross: a record of bodily suffering and death. The intent is to liberate the head or mind from the body for contemplation of the divine. Accordingly, words (incantations, prayers, hymns) become the dominant form of experience, continuing Cabiria's progress beyond the visible. The images that appear (in contrast to those at Lazzari's) tend to be evocative or mandalic rather than representative: mere outlines or hollow symmetrical forms which one looks through as well as at. When they are representative, they refer to spiritual rather than physical reality (e.g., the picture of Madonna and Child to which Cabiria prays).

Within this environment, Cabiria becomes cerebral for the first time. She isolates herself from the picnickers following the pilgrimage, states "I'm thinking," and contemplates the apparent failure of the pilgrimage to effect transformation. (The only thing she consumes is some wine, which goes, appropriately, right to her *head!*) More important, though it is not clear until the following sequence, Cabiria acquires a crucial mental tool— the symbol of the Virgin Mary—to assist her in her attempts to change. One of the principal incantatory phrases at the shrine is "Viva Maria," a phrase that is also electrified and elevated as a dominant visual sign. Under hypnosis at the Lux, Cabiria will take the name "Maria" as a way of articulating her quest for renewal and her journey beyond prostitution.

At the end of the picnic scene, Cabiria's urge for transformation removes her from a shared and familiar world. She rejects the company of her friends. She also rejects the institutionalized religious quest that she has been part of—violently mocking a group of pilgrims off in a field. Yet even as she mocks them, she looks longingly after them, with regret that she is no longer part of their search. Her pilgrim eyes make clear that, though she has abandoned the quests of orthodoxy, she has not abandoned the quest per se. And, as the procession becomes ever smaller in the distance, it draws Cabiria's vision even closer to the vanishing point than did the procession at the Passeggiata. She is now on the verge of a personal pilgrimage that will take her beyond the given world, into the realm of creative fantasy.

This occurs at the Lux theater, whose name and fiercely illuminating spotlight establish it as a source of symbolic enlightenment. At the Lux, Cabiria shuts her eyes to reality and withdraws completely into her mind and imagination.

Two of the more important things featured here are magnetism and miracles. Magnetism, a power of attraction so intense that one person can enter and influence another's mind, is a model of extraordinary spiritual affinity. Though it is employed manipulatively by the Conjuror, its true potential is redeemed and actualized by Cabiria in her imagined love relation to Oscar. Miracles appear largely as metamorphosis: the Conjuror turns male head into female, woman into ape, a stage and a bench (through hypnotic suggestion) into a voyage at sea. Cabiria has entered a world where anything can seemingly become anything else and where her Divine Love dream of radical change can be fulfilled.

In going to the Lux, Cabiria has done something both new and entirely on her own for the first time. She has abandoned prostitution, at least for this evening. She has, in a limited sense, "gone away," as she predicted she would at the picnic. Her growing independence is confirmed by her experience here. Instead of being exposed to merely conventional and external solutions to the problem of self-fulfillment (e.g., movie stars and religion), she discovers the redemptive powers that have been growing within her.

Cabiria's independence can also be seen in her changing relation to the Conjuror. At first he dominates her, putting her in and out of hypnosis at will. However, when the topic of Oscar is introduced, Cabiria in a subtle but crucial way *chooses* to become entranced.[5] As the Maria-Oscar story unfolds, she gradually takes over: picking flowers, inventing dialogue, and making the Conjuror, in his role as Oscar, respond to her rather than vice versa. Finally, she becomes so active and powerful in her role that she startles the Conjuror, putting him on the defensive and forcing him to end the trance.

The full extent of Cabiria's growth becomes clear from the nature and content of the Maria-Oscar tale. The Conjuror describes it as a feat of

Cabiria begins her interior journey toward a vision of love and the discovery of an ideal self at the Lux Theatre. Courtesy: Museum of Modern Art/Film Stills Archive.

"auto-suggestion"—"self-suggestion"—and the phrase is even more accurate than the Conjuror intends. In identifying and acknowledging her innermost dreams, Cabiria "suggests" or creates an ideal self, "Maria." She creates the basis for a self-love and self-acceptance which, when fully realized, will allow her to face life in even its most threatening aspects. Her growing faith is reflected here in her willingness to open out completely to the imagined Oscar.

As Cabiria grows in her capacity for transformation, she must come to accept death as part of a unitive vision of life. Consistent with this, the stage at the Lux confronts Cabiria with images of decapitation, skulls, and stopped clocks; and just prior to the Maria-Oscar trance, the Conjuror hypnotizes several men into a vision of shipwreck. Death, however, is no longer a physical threat for Cabiria; the shipwreck re-creates Cabiria's near drowning earlier on the level of fantasy.

Even more important, Cabiria undergoes two imaginative "deaths" and "rebirths" during the sequence. First, she dies off as Cabiria (through hypnosis) to become Maria. Then she dies as Maria to become a new Cabiria. The latter is especially significant. When the Conjuror brings the trance to an end, Cabiria/"Maria" slumps unconscious to the floor, and before he can bend all the way down to assist her, she pops up, reawakened. Again, the opening scenes are recalled—but Cabiria can now bring herself back to life without male intervention.

Cabiria's development through the Lux sequence, though extraordinary, is incomplete. It requires her withdrawal from reality, her escape into fantasy. It is also largely unreflective. Rather than being truly conscious of what she is doing, Cabiria tends merely to sense inadequacies or possibilities in response to what happens to her. This is clear even in her most cerebral of moments—at the picnic—where her promise to sell everything and go away is more a momentary outburst of confused emotion than a lucid, rational decision. (Accordingly, she fails to follow through completely on her promise till late in the movie.) Following the Lux, Cabiria must reconnect with the tangible and concrete. She must develop a formative and fully conscious intelligence that can act upon the given, transform it, and create the conditions necessary for spiritual fulfillment.

Cabiria's first encounter with the "real" Oscar is quite pointedly associated with a return to reality. She stands in the Lux lobby after the show, refusing to go outside and face some lingering male hecklers. When the cleaning woman insists that she must, Cabiria finally exits, and Oscar materializes virtually out of the wall of a building. He immediately begins to function as Cabiria's bridge back from the ideal to the real as he explains to Cabiria what she did under hypnosis and thus externalizes her fantasies for her.

Their first meeting also establishes Oscar's role as a stimulant for Cabiria's practical intelligence. He introduces himself as a *ragioniere*—an accountant or, in its root sense, a "reasoner"—and throughout their first scenes together he repeatedly accounts for Cabiria's experiences with rational explanations. Early in their relationship, he serves largely as her surrogate intelligence, but she quickly makes his powers of reason her own.

Oscar is also a consummate role-player. Capable of completely disguising his fraudulent nature, he is by far the most metamorphic, the most self-transformative, figure Cabiria encounters. Even more important, the role he adopts serves as the final bridge for Cabiria between prostitution and love. He presents himself as an unconditional giver, who asks nothing in return for his kindness and generosity. He talks repeatedly in terms of empathy and profound understanding. In making no demands on Cabiria, he allows her to be what she wants to be—encouraging her to pursue all her finest inclinations. Offered both a model of perfect love and the freedom to develop her own giving instincts, Cabiria becomes increasingly open, loving, and trusting. The result is suggested by Oscar's own words: "when we are suddenly faced with purity and candor, then the mask of cynicism falls. All that is best in us is awakened." Moreover, by the time Oscar reveals his true intent, Cabiria has developed the spiritual strength to neutralize him, and to live beyond the need for him.

With the appearance of Oscar, Cabiria begins another cycle of growth beyond physical and material reality, though on a much higher level than before. In her first two scenes with Oscar, she is content to be a mere recipient of gifts. As she says to Wanda: "Who cares, as long as he pays?" (Her reference to money suggests that her relationship at this point is merely another form of prostitution.) However, when she is nearly arrested at the Passeggiata, she has a moment of awakening similar to when she asked herself "What if I'd died?" She realizes that prostitution is a dead end, and she begins to view Oscar as the bridge to a new life. No longer a mere fact of life to be accepted unquestioningly, Oscar becomes a possibility, a means to an end.

During the next several scenes, Cabiria becomes much more active and responsive, and her responsiveness is linked to a growing capacity for intense thought. Her scene of awakened concern at the Passeggiata is followed by one of pensive attention as she listens to Oscar recount his presumed personal history. This is followed by a scene in which Cabiria, home alone, slowly rises from bed, leaves her house, and wanders down the road, lost in meditation. Born out of her thoughts are the otherworldly voice and image of Brother Giovanni. A virtual apparition, he brings revelation from the realm of spirit: telling Cabiria that she must be in the grace of God to be happy and that she should be married because "matrimony is a holy thing." His words alter radically Cabiria's relationship to

Oscar. She no longer views him solely as a vehicle of escape from the Passeggiata; in fact, her initial response is to tell him that she will not see him any more. From here on, she insists on spiritual rather than utilitarian value. She wants the holiness of full union or nothing at all, and she comes to view Oscar as nothing less than a potential source of grace. She thus relates to Oscar both as a person and as a symbol, combining the real and the ideal.

Moreover, in accepting Oscar's offer of marriage, she comes to see transformation in terms of movement beyond self and movement beyond all that is known and familiar. She prepares to give up prostitution, to sell her house, and to leave behind the maternal Wanda. True, she appears to be doing all this for Oscar, but—as becomes clear by the end—he is not an embodiment of the familiar. He is the absolute "Other," the denial of all Cabiria has been.

As Cabiria comes to view Oscar in spiritual and symbolic terms, he temporarily disappears as a character. He is absent from five of six scenes in which Cabiria makes crucial decisions and takes crucial actions regarding her life. Though she does not realize it, she has already supplanted salvation through Oscar with self-liberation.

Her competence, decisiveness, and self-confidence are evident in the scene of packing and departure, when it becomes clear that she has made arrangements for everything (sale of the house, disposal of goods, withdrawal of money). Moreover, by the time she walks out the front door and surrenders the keys to her house (a film-long refuge and image of closure), she is completely opened out. She tries to communicate with everyone she is leaving behind. She expresses immense love for Wanda—love so strong that even Wanda abandons her habitual coolness and responds in kind. As she awaits the bus, she is able to balance both profound joy (the anticipation of union with Oscar) and profound sorrow (the pain of losing Wanda and severing all ties with the past). As she bids Wanda good-bye, she assures Wanda that she too will experience a "miracle"—revealing that she now sees her life as miraculous and is thus prepared for religious transformation.

Cabiria's spiritual and moral power is such that she dominates Oscar during their final scenes. She overwhelms him with her openness—forcing him repeatedly to retreat behind his dark jacket and dark glasses. She has reversed their relationship since their meeting outside the Lux. She has, in fact, *become* Oscar to the extent that she has assimilated all his positive qualities. She says as much, without realizing it, when she tells him they are *uguali*—a word which means not only "equal" but "the same" or "identical."

Even after she has discovered Oscar's real intentions, she remains dominant. The power of her fear and disillusionment drives Oscar to defensive silence. More than that, it partially redeems him. Not only can he not

*Her expression growing ever softer and more luminous, Cabiria be-
comes an unconditional lover as she offers all her savings to Oscar.*

bring himself to kill her, he is turned from murderer into savior as he pulls
Cabiria away from the brink and says "Can't you see, I don't want to hurt
you." Furthermore, he does not actually rob her. He only takes the money
she drops at his feet as an offering—money which is no longer of value to
her.

Obviously, Cabiria's confrontation with Oscar reenacts her near drowning at the hands of Giorgio. In contrast with the opening scene, where
physical well-being was the issue, spiritual health is at stake here. Cabiria
is challenged with the destruction of all external sources of faith, love,
hope, and grace. Her ability to recover and endure, moved by a grace of
her own creation, is far more significant than her earlier capacity for resurrection at the hands of others. The fact that Cabiria's activity takes place
on a much higher moral and spiritual plane is reflected in the location of
the action far above sea level. The water, which was an immediate and
tangible threat in the opening scene, is now distant: symbolic of an en-
gulfment far more profound than drowning.

Most important, Cabiria *chooses* her "death" here. At the moment of
revelation, she sees herself as though through Oscar's eyes (there is an

extreme closeup of those eyes from her point of view), and she sees herself as someone of no account, a creature worth only her dowry. At that moment, all remaining egoism, all false sense of worth is destroyed, and Cabiria becomes willing to die. She tells Oscar "Kill me. Throw me in. I don't want to live." Though she does not realize it, what she is seeking is the death that precedes enlightenment—the death of all she has ever been, so that she can be reborn anew.

This occurs once Oscar has gone. She gradually lapses into unconsciousness, and as she does her sobs become those of a little girl, her final cry that of a baby. She then lies dormant, at a moment prior to infancy, prior to birth, about to awaken to a moral environment so highly evolved that Oscar and all he embodies are no longer possible.

Cabiria's death is the moment of final transcendence beyond simple identity, "selfhood"—that sense of separate, alienated individuality that was born the moment she confronted her mortality. As she comes back to life in the final scene, picks up the bouquet she had gathered earlier, and moves back through the woods, Cabiria becomes a bride of life: married to no one in particular but to the world at large. Her willingness to keep on keeping on, despite her recent devastation, generates the youngsters whose music and dance celebrate their life and hers. Though their appearance is miraculous, it is not arbitrary. They are her own transcendent powers released into the world, her own capacity for resurrection and renewal acting upon her in a spiritual domain where all separation between self and world has vanished.

Brief as it is, the final sequence recapitulates all the major processes of the film. Cabiria moves from alienation to engagement. Male dominance (among the youths) gives way to female liberation. Most important, body gives way to spirit, weight to lightness. When Cabiria awakens, her movements are ponderous, and even when she begins to walk, she is leaden and slow. However, she becomes increasingly fluid as she mingles with the youngsters. At the moment she is bid *Buona sera* and restored in spirit, her materiality—and that of her world—vanishes. In the final images there is no road, no bouquet (the last of Cabiria's "possessions" to disappear), no "world's body." There is only the enlightened image of Cabiria's face and upper body, floating weightlessly in space, absorbing and releasing the upper-body images of the youths who float behind her. They, in turn, are present only through rear projection, which makes them lighter and larger than life.

In performing their vital restorative service, Cabiria's companions function in an extraordinarily complex way. Their youthfulness provides Cabiria with a model of newness, hence *re*newal (Fellini has described them as "humanity on the threshold of life").[6] Their actions and movement bespeak a world in which all motion has become dance, all sound music, all life harmony.[7] Their orderly yet spontaneous progression reenacts all the many processions that have occurred before. The boys in the group rein-carnate the adolescents who saved Cabiria. They also redeem the pimps from the Passeggiata and recall the nightclub musicians from the Lazzari sequence. The girls, of course, are the redemption of prostitution, the recovery of innocence. The dark-haired girl who says *Buona sera* clearly incarnates "Maria" from the Lux and resurrects Cabiria as an adolescent. (As Oscar and Cabiria left the seaside restaurant, Cabiria remarked "You should have seen me when I was fifteen. I had long black hair down to here.") She is another manifestation of Cabiria's transcendent self released into the world.

In responding radiantly to the words *Buona sera*, Cabiria confirms that the unknown has been redeemed from terror. In a world of loving relat-edness, the "evening" has indeed—and finally—become good. Though the darkness will come, the nights of Cabiria will forever be redeemed by the light of the spirit.

As Cabiria comes to accept the evening and all it signifies, she becomes a figure of extraordinary vision, caressing all with her accepting gaze. She becomes both a luminous moving image and an image who sees lumi-nously on the move. Not only do Cabiria's eyes embrace the visible, they see into the heart of the unseen. Just before the film ends, her eyes focus briefly on the camera eye. Cabiria has discovered the unseen source of creation: the "divine" power that has given her life. She acknowledges it not as something on which she depends, but as something *uguale*. It too is a reflection of herself poured into the world.

In seeing into the camera eye, Cabiria also sees into the eyes and souls of the viewers—destroying the conventional mediation between spectator and film. In piercing the veil of invisibility, Cabiria does not end up in the realm of illusion as she did at the Lux. She connects with powers (camera eye and us) that are indeed present though not seen by her. This becomes the final and fullest expression of her capacity to live in a universe of spirit—a universe defined by the paradoxical presentness of absence, which can only be experienced through the genius of seeing what is there yet invisible.

The Nights of Cabiria and Fellini's Imaginative Development

As we suggested at the conclusion of the last chapter, *The Nights of Cabiria* is the natural outgrowth of *Il Bidone*. It gives form to the world beyond tragedy promised by *Il Bidone*'s closing images. Moreover, the character of Cabiria continues a progression in individuality and assertive-ness that can be traced from the ultradependent and conventional Checco, Ivan, and Wanda, through the aggressive isolate Zampanò, to the

As Cabiria gazes into our eyes, she is a marvelously unified image. Her face, which is teared yet smiling, unites water and light—two elements that throughout the film have been juxtaposed as part of a death-life dichotomy. Her teared smile also combines sorrow and joy, pain and pleasure, tragedy and comedy. The spot of wet mascara that stains her face beneath her left eye redeems the prominent mole near Oscar's right eye. Her stained image implies that she is a woman of experience as well as of renewed innocence, an adult as well as a child. The resurrected and revitalized Cabiria carries everything forward in synthesis.

artist of his own demise, Augusto. Unlike Zampanò and Augusto, Cabiria can combine a "feminine" talent for wholeness with the "masculine" urge for differentiation. In addition, she takes all the energy that earlier Fellini characters had turned against themselves and makes it work toward her liberation.

By seeing Cabiria through to liberation, Fellini seems to have liberated something within himself. Following *The Nights of Cabiria*, his films have a richness and explosive power only hinted at in the earlier work. It seems that with Cabiria (and again through the magical inspiration of Giulietta Masina) he has freed his imagination more than ever to live in the creation.

9

La Dolce Vita

La Dolce Vita (1960) derived from two major sources: "Moraldo in the City"—a project which, as we noted earlier, Fellini had contemplated after *I Vitelloni*[1]—and Fellini's personal impressions of the Via Veneto, which had recently become a famous international hangout for the trendy. The film was enormously controversial and enormously successful—with the furor it raised contributing to its box office appeal. Partly because of the outrage it triggered among the Italian clergy, *La Dolce Vita* acquired a reputation as a scandalous celebration of decadence. (This all seems quite absurd from the perspective of the 1980s.) Moreover, the film helped highlight the perpetual division in Italy between Catholicism and Marxism. While much of the Catholic intelligentsia found the film irreligious and prurient, the Marxists applauded it as a stunning indictment of bourgeois society.

Partly because of the attention it received and largely because of its integrity and power—which seem all the more evident today as the memory of controversy dims—*La Dolce Vita* has done much to confirm Fellini's reputation, not only in the world of film but in the broader context of Western literary tradition. With the film's release, comparisons with Dante, T. S. Eliot, and other major writers past and present began to appear with frequency in discussions of Fellini's work.

Like *The Nights of Cabiria*, *La Dolce Vita* is vitally concerned with religious and spiritual patterns of experience. However, unlike *Cabiria* (except for a final and quite crucial moment of redemption), *La Dolce Vita* tends to focus on the inability of people to spiritualize their lives. Characters repeatedly, though unwittingly, avoid the challenge of growth by escaping into purely sensual activity. This is reflected both in the film's title and in the heavy emphasis on unfulfilling sexuality. As with *The Nights of Cabiria*, we must distinguish Fellini's religious or spiritual vision from that of orthodox Catholicism. *La Dolce Vita* is not a diatribe against the senses, an implicit endorsement of renunciation. It envisions a society in which healthy sensuality is absent. Moreover, like *La Strada*, it is a film of failed

The "Second Coming": a statue of Christ is ferried toward St. Peter's by helicopter at the beginning of La Dolce Vita.

evolution in which characters are unable to grow from physical to imaginative life. They fail not because they refuse to deny bodily existence but because they are unable to make it the starting point for more complex forms of experience.

The film's emphasis on sexuality is related to the characters' need for renewal through love, a need suggested in the opening scene by the Second-Coming image of Christ, in a gesture of loving embrace, being whisked "back" to the world by helicopter. Maddalena, who wants a "whole new life,"[2] substitutes nymphomania for more valid forms of engagement. Marcello pursues Maddalena and Sylvia as sources of romantic salvation. Emma prays at the miracle site for the renewal of Marcello's love. Marcello's father tries to recapture lost youth by courting a woman thirty years younger. Both the passion for renewal and the inability of characters to achieve it give *La Dolce Vita* its profoundly tragic dimension.

The brief opening sequence of *La Dolce Vita* introduces the crucial problem of false spirituality. The power of flight ("transcendence") is mechanized—possessed only by a couple of whirlybirds. The image of Spirit and Love (Christ) is rigid, heavy, bound for earth, and mechanically controlled. Both the spiritual reawakening and renewal promised by a Second Coming are destined to fail. The impossibility of the former is suggested humorously when the statue of Christ actually *does* trigger an "awakening" of four female sunbathers, who respond by saying "It's Jesus Christ" (*DV*, 2). Obviously, it is *not* Christ, it is just a statue, and the women are displacing spirituality onto a physical object or symbol. The impossibility of renewal is indicated by the absence or disappearance of vital sources, both physical and spiritual. Water is conspicuously missing from the ruined aqueducts. "Christ" never lands.

The imagery of the Second Coming suggests a world awaiting salvation from without because the capacity for self-redemption has been lost. The theatrical effect of the statue's appearance points to a society in which spectacle has replaced more spiritual forms of renewal—a world which relies on movie stars, media, and gossip journalism to rescue it from boredom.

Marcello's situation is rapidly sketched for us. Caught between a petrified image of spiritual love and more vital physical alternatives, he is moved toward the latter as his helicopter abandons Christ for the sunbathers. He is also caught (as his profession would suggest) in a world of mere observation. Everything meaningful remains outside him. Moreover, he is divided between professional duty (covering the "Second Coming") and personal inclination (chasing women). This division is also one between "spirit" and "body"—reflecting a world hopelessly polarized, as well as one in which the spirit is associated not with personal experience but with work. Finally, when the sunbathers respond with an emphatic "No" to a request for their phone numbers, Marcello is exposed for the first time to negation or denial as an appropriate response to life. (Here we recall *I Vitelloni* and the fact that Marcello is, in some ways, "Moraldo in the City.")

Though neither helicopter lands, the camera eye does. The final shot reveals St. Peter's Square, concluding a movement from the celestial airiness of the opening moments, through increasingly earthbound images, as the camera eye is drawn toward the center of Rome. The grounding of the camera eye is paralleled by the downward thrust of Marcello's vision. We never see him look up at the statue of Christ. He looks down at the sunbathers on the roof, then, the last time we see him in the sequence, he looks over the side of the helicopter and straight down to earth. Unlike Cabiria, he has no capacity for looking beyond the immediate, seeing beyond the seen. Instead he is victim to a gravitational pull that eventually captures everyone except Paola, and reduces the Second Coming to an inexorable descent.

The first major phase of the film extends from Marcello's evening with Maddalena through his attempts to write at the beach. Marcello tries to move beyond his given world and to discover greater intellectual and spiritual significance in his life. His efforts are reflected in his attempted abandonment of journalism (reporting on existing reality) for "literature" (creating a world apart). They are also evident in his increasingly ethereal relation to women and the feminine—from having sex with Maddalena to worshipping the sex goddess Sylvia, then to investigating the possible apparition of the Blessed Mother and to viewing Paola as an "Umbrian angel."

Marcello is exposed to the same stages of development as was Cabiria. In the opening scene, he is just an unself-conscious respondent to events, at the mercy of his job, his helicopter, and life in general. When Maddalena appears, she brings with her an intense sense of self-awareness—talking of her alienation, her desire to be separate and alone. This recalls Cabiria's self-consciousness at the Passeggiata Archeologica and the Via Veneto, as well as Matilde's remark "Notice the difference between me and all of you." Marcello himself experiences a moment of potential awakening when he is shocked into full alertness (and shot in the most extreme closeup in the film) upon discovering the overdosed Emma. His response parallels Cabiria's question, "What if I'd died?" Then, with the introduction of the movie star Sylvia, Marcello is moved to visual astonishment, projection, romantic wonder, and idealization, just as Cabiria was with Lazzari. Sylvia's appearance is followed by a brief scene in church (with Steiner) and by Marcello's visit to the miracle site—which correspond with the brief procession scene at the Passeggiata, followed by the pil-grimage, in *Cabiria*. (In each case, the main character is ushered into the realm of the invisible and spiritual.) Then, just as Cabiria visited the Lux, where she could escape completely into her mind, Marcello visits the home of Steiner—a disembodied intellectual who lives in a world of phi-losophy and art. Cabiria's absorption in the fictional tale of Maria and Os-car becomes Marcello's attempts to create "literature" (presumably fiction) by the sea.

Unlike Cabiria, Marcello is unable to internalize these stages of poten-tial enlightenment. The contrast with Cabiria becomes quite pointed when we see that certain events which occurred *to* or *through* Cabiria only occur *outside* Marcello. (Again, Marcello's extravert profession as re-porter helps define his dilemma.) For instance, Cabiria's drowning and resuscitation—her "death and rebirth"—become Emma's attempted sui-cide and recovery. Likewise, Cabiria's "What if I'd died?" becomes Mar-cello's confrontation not with his own mortality but with Emma's. And during the religious scenes it is Emma who prays for a miracle, not Mar-cello. Because all remains externalized, Marcello fails to develop Madda-lena's acute self-awareness, his idealization of Sylvia never gets beyond childish dependency, he cannot create spiritual value at the miracle, and he relies on Steiner as a surrogate intelligence. Inevitably, he is unable to create anything when left to his own intellectual devices at the beach.

Not only does consciousness fail to evolve, but every sequence moves to an outright denial of enlightenment. First, when Marcello discovers Emma (who has, in effect, killed off her own consciousness), his intense concern and fear suggest that he is on the verge of an awakening. How-ever, at the hospital, when Emma is out of danger and he has the oppor-tunity to contemplate what has happened (as Cabiria contemplated her near drowning), he refuses to do so. Instead, he calls Maddalena, whose dead-to-the-world image externalizes Marcello's inability to awaken or be reborn.

Second, though Sylvia sparks a temporary increase in Marcello's mental activity, she herself is utterly lacking in powers of intellect or self-con-sciousness, and she ultimately leads Marcello to close his eyes and lose himself both in the waters of the Trevi and in her amnesic embrace. Mar-cello even verbalizes his denial of consciousness when, in reverence for Sylvia's purely sensate, nonreflective behavior, he proclaims: "Yes, yes, she's perfectly right. I've been wrong about everything" (*DV*, 79).

Third, unlike Cabiria, who attended the Divine Love pilgrimage out of personal interest and aspiration, Marcello visits the miracle site solely in his role as reporter—and at no time during the sequence does he show the slightest sign of emerging religious sensibility. Moreover, he is absent for the one moment when genuine religious intuition is present—when

Sylvia's earlier arrival by plane marked another "Second Coming" in
La Dolce Vita. *Here she is about to be joined by Marcello in the engulf-*
ing waters of the Trevi fountain.

Marianne tells Emma that actual appearances by the Madonna are not
what count, it is the individual's capacity to draw on all the spiritual influences that inevitably surround one.[3]

As daylight gives way to darkness, all spiritual possibility is eliminated.
The Madonna fails to appear, the quest for revelation is replaced by the
destruction of the "miracle tree," and a pilgrim dies—his prayers mani-
festly unanswered. Within this context, the words of a woman shouting
"he's dead, he's dead" (*DV*, 11) seem to refer as much to the death of God
as to the death of the pilgrim. The dawn returns, as it will so many times
in the film, to illuminate only the emptiness.

Fourth, Steiner, who as an intellectual should be a vital force for the
development of consciousness, contributes instead to its destruction. Suffering from characteristic intellectual paranoia in the face of reality, he
dreams of eternal escape: "We need to live in a state of suspended anima-
tion, like a work of art. In a state of enchantment. We have to . . . live
outside time, detached" (S). As we suggested in discussing the nun's the-

ological premises in *La Strada*, this kind of detachment denies the responsibility of a truly awakened relation to life. Steiner, in effect, is using his intellect to negate itself. His words here are his last in the film, and thus provide the link to his final act—shooting himself in the head—which is both a symbolic and an irredeemably real denial of consciousness.

The fifth, and final, denial occurs with Marcello's abandonment of writing at the beach. Not only is he unable to live in the realm of purely mental invention, he cannot find inspiration from spiritualized reality (the angelic image of Paola). Instead, he reverts to Emma, whose physicality is emphatically visualized as she sprawls across the bed to answer Marcello's call admitting defeat.

During the first phase of *La Dolce Vita* there is a discernible progression from physical, bodily experience (Marcello's relation with Maddalena, Emma's illness) to idealization of the physical (Marcello's pursuit of Sylvia), to transcendence of the physical through spirit or imagination (the miracle site, where the Madonna is wholly invented and conspicuous by her physical absence), to attempted imaginative self-transformation (Marcello at the beach, seeking to evolve into a creative writer). Not only does this parallel (albeit negatively) Cabiria's movement from Giorgio to Lazzari to the Divine Love pilgrimage to the Lux, it recurs as a basic pattern in the second phase of *La Dolce Vita*. The sequence with Marcello's father is one of sexual and bodily experience (his illness even parallels Emma's). Then, at the Castle, idealization takes over as Marcello—left in the Chamber of Serious Discourse—rhapsodizes over Maddalena. Idealization is replaced by forms of spiritual transcendence as aristocrats engage in a ghost hunt or "pilgrimage" which ends in a seance and is followed by a dawn procession to Mass. Finally, back at the birthplace of his own quest for self-transformation—Steiner's apartment—Marcello encounters the corpse of Steiner, who has chosen his own nihilistic form of "self-transformation" through suicide.

Obviously, in each case the second-phase version is a radical diminishment of the first. Marcello himself does not share in emotional or sexual experience with Fanny—he merely functions as a voyeur as his father tries to recapture his past. (In fact, Marcello unconsciously uses Fanny as a go-between, so that he does not have to relate intimately with his father.) Marcello's worship of Maddalena is even more desperate and comic than his pursuit of Sylvia, given Maddalena's clear lack of all the virtues he imparts to her. The ghost hunt and seance debase the desire for the Madonna and spiritual revitalization that motivated at least some of the visitors to the miracle site. And Steiner's killing of himself and his children is a violent renunciation of meaningful change or self-renewal.

Each of these instances is part of a larger, more encompassing diminishment in the film's moral climate. Through much of the first phase there

was a strong sense of possibility. Marcello sought new modes of experience through his relationships with Sylvia and Steiner, and the pilgrims at
the miracle site sought divine revelation. During the second phase possibility is replaced by mere givenness, the challenge to create something
new becomes merely the attempt to respond to what is already there.
Concomitantly, while the first phase moved to the denial of *creative*
consciousness, the second culminates in the death of merely *responsive*
consciousness, and while the first revealed the meaninglessness of the
possible, the second discloses the sterility of the given.

The substitution of givenness for possibility is immediately suggested
by Marcello's return to dependency on Emma at the end of the beach
scene—and by his return to mere reporting and his "beat" at the Via Veneto in succeeding sequences. It is even more profoundly present in several fundamental shifts that occur within the film.

For one thing, the past replaces the future and dominates the present.
This change has been signaled by Steiner, whose cultivation of Sanskrit
and Bach was an attempt to avoid the future: "The world will be wonderful
they say. But from whose viewpoint, if one phone call can announce the
end of everything?" (S).

From the opening moments of the second phase, Marcello is in the
hands of characters from either a personal or a cultural past who cannot
accept life in the present. His father maintains "with age things get worse"
(*DV*, 173), rhapsodizes about the good old days, and tries to recapture
them by revisiting an old night spot. Prince Mascalchi—a member of the
aging and decaying aristocracy—bemoans the fact that "everything [is]
falling to pieces" (*DV*, 204). The aristocracy sequence moves relentlessly
backward in time, from the present-day world of Rome and the Via Veneto
to the Castle of Bassano di Sutri, then to a dilapidated 500-year-old villa
where the guests try to make contact with spirits of the dead. Steiner, in
killing his children and then committing suicide, abrogates the present
and future and makes the past absolute.

Consistent with this, the only major new figure Marcello meets during
this phase—the painter Jane—is a walking denial of newness. As an American, a "blonde" (her hair is streaked), and a visual artist, she initially offers
some promise of reincarnating Sylvia, whose new world vitality and repeated association with the song *Arrivederci, Roma* made her a potential
force for renewal. However, Jane is a prisoner of the past. Not only has
she chosen to live in Rome, but she becomes the standard-bearer of the
dying aristocracy—the leader of the ghost hunt to the ruined villa.

As the predominance of the past eliminates the possibility for creative
change, spirit—the vital source of newness, evolution, and so on—is even
further supplanted by physical, material, substitutes. (This is implied
right at the start of the second phase when *Il Papa*—the pope and spiritual
father to whom the statue of Christ was being delivered in the film's open-

ing scene—is replaced by the mere biological *papa* of Marcello.) During the Castle sequence, as Marcello tries to idealize Maddalena, she abandons him in the "Chamber of Serious Discourse" and starts necking with one of the guests. The "pilgrimage" to the villa and the ensuing seance give way to nymphomania, as Federica proves possessed not by any spirit but by lust for Giulio. Finally, defeated by the emptiness of experience, Marcello surrenders to casual—virtually arbitrary—sex with Jane.

The most shocking replacement of spirit occurs through the reappearance of the once ethereal Steiner as a mere corpse. His lifeless body becomes the second in a series of three images—the statue of Christ, the dead Steiner, and the monstrous fish at the end—which punctuate a film-long devolution from (false) spiritual possibility to brute matter.

With all sense of possibility gone, Marcello is helpless to initiate change. He functions increasingly as a follower and as a character thrust into preexisting situations. He has to be told by his co-workers of his father's presence at the Via Veneto. He relies on Nico to take him to the Castle, where he is captured and dragged around by Maddalena. Abandoned by her, he is swept up by the ghost hunt. Finally, he is captured yet again—this time by Jane—in the midst of Federica's sexual seizure. Even during his fight with Emma, though he appears to be assertive, he is actually reacting to demands that she is making on him. Finally, he has to be awakened out of a deep sleep in order to be informed of Steiner's death.

By this point, he is barely able to react to experience, much less create it, and his visit to the scene of Steiner's death not only confirms the loss of creative consciousness, it marks the end of responsive intelligence. The apartment is crowded with detectives whose only mode of operation is to measure, record, and analyze what is dead (irrevocably "given"). They admit utter helplessness in trying to determine motive (the spiritual or intellectual source of Steiner's actions). Mind is reduced to bureaucratic machinery.

Marcello himself is in a state of shock (a "response" which, as we saw with Gelsomina, is actually a denial of response). When questioned by the police, all he can say is: "I don't know anything. I really don't know anything." "I don't think so." "I don't know." (*DV*, 226–27) Even the one seemingly active thing he does—accompany the police to the bus stop in order to identify Mrs. Steiner—serves to emphasize his inability rather than his ability to respond. He is too numb to comply with the commissioner's request that he tell the *paparazzi* not to harass Anna. Moreover, though he is presumably acting in a personal capacity (Anna is a friend), he acts only as a *reporter*, pointing out her arrival. He makes no effort to speak with or console her, and he merely acquiesces in the police commissioner's lie that her children are only wounded.

Actually, Marcello is even less than a reporter here, for reporting entails some re-creation. He is mainly a "camera" that registers external happenings. The analogy is suggested by Fellini in the final shot of the second phase: an extreme closeup of Paparazzo's camera, which asserts the prevalence of merely replicative, dead-eye vision in a world from which both formative and engaged intelligence have vanished. (This closeup, in turn, dissolves into a shot of headlights—more mechanical "eyes.")

The Annulment Party

By now all meaning, all basis for affirmation or involvement, has been eliminated. Accordingly, the sequence following Steiner's death is a party celebrating not only the annulment of a marriage (i.e., love, relatedness) but, as Marcello puts it, "the annulment of everything" (*DV*, 236).

Annulment implies the death of renewal (it wipes out without replacing), and the party turns into a brutally self-destructive parody of regeneration. Intended to celebrate Nadia's newfound freedom and her "becoming a virgin again" (*DV*, 236–37), it shows only her dependence on a new lover and a worldweariness that is the very opposite of innocence. More profoundly, the party denigrates the promise of renewal once offered by Christianity. Christmas is associated either with murder (one character predicts that two homosexuals will be killed before Christmas) or with banality (the homosexuals dance to a hideous version of *Jingle Bells*). Sacraments of cleansing and/or of preparation for a new life are mimicked and debased—a process which culminates with Marcello's violent dousing and slapping of Pasutt. Her "baptism" and "confirmation" are accompanied by a vicious mockery of self-transformation, as she is turned into a chicken, with pillow feathers, by Marcello. The sequence concludes with a benediction of sorts, as Marcello showers the departing guests with feathers. His actions make a procession out of their departure into a new day, but the ritual here is as meaningless as were Zampanò's and Picasso's baptisms in *La Strada* and *Il Bidone*.

With both creative consciousness and responsive intelligence destroyed, Marcello and his companions demonstrate the very negative of intelligent behavior: a drunken outpouring of repressed, nihilistic energy. This kind of anticonsciousness mocks and repudiates true intelligence. Marcello—sardonically designated the party "intellectual"—brags of his inventiveness: "I have a thousand, two thousand ideas" (*DV*, 252), but his "ideas" are solely and debasedly sexual in nature. (Mind or spirit is again sacrificed to hollow sexuality.) Concomitantly, the only form of idealization left is drunken admiration of Nadia's naked body.

Marcello's repeated, mindless slapping of Pasutt is part of an all-out assault on the head through which characters express their antipathy toward conscious life. Marcello tosses a drink in Laura's face. Lisa draws a caricature of Marcello's head on a glass ball which Marcello proceeds to smash with a whiskey bottle. His new boss, Sernas, slams Marcello in the face with a pillow and, shortly thereafter, grabs him in a headlock. Marcello not only douses and slaps Pasutt's face, he pounds her over the head repeatedly with a pillow. (As a dumb blonde, Pasutt negates all the light-haired women before her—Sylvia, Paola, and even Nico—who were associated with the possible, though increasingly unlikely, awakening of consciousness.)

Marcello's crucial role in the festivities proves only to be an occasion for self-annulment. (His urge to repudiate himself is immediately suggested when he appears in a white suit and black tie that are the "negative" of his evening attire earlier in the film.) His brutalization of Pasutt is largely self-brutalization, for he sees her as a reflection of himself.[4] His destruction of the glass caricature is a denial of what little identity he has left. His new job—publicity agent for a vacuous movie star—is a self-contemptuous denial of his earlier intellectual aspirations. In the course of the evening, he drowns his compromised intelligence in alcohol, becoming less and less coherent and reducing himself to a bleary-eyed state.

The Beach: Marcello

As the party comes to an end and the guests leave the annulment villa, the process of moral and spiritual depletion is complete. "I've lost all interest in this life" (*DV*, 268), proclaims Domino as he walks with Marcello—speaking for Marcello and everyone else. Marcello, in turn, reacts to the enormous dead fish which seems to be staring at him by saying: "What is there for it to look at?" (T).

The exhausted revellers' brief journey back to the sea recalls Zampanò's at the end of *La Strada*. Like his, it is a final regression to the origins of evolution, after evolution has failed. The monstrous fish, reflecting the state of Marcello's society, is an image of brute matter devoid of spirit. Dragged up from the sea, it—like Augusto's struggle up the hill in *Il Bidone*—exemplifies meaningless ascent. In Jungian terms, it suggests the impossibility of transition from unconscious life (the sea) to consciousness (the shore, the light of dawn).

In apocalyptic terms, the fish suggests the death of Christ, the death of Christianity. "Icythus," the Greek word for fish, was used in early Christianity to designate the Savior, and, in this instance, the fish is specifically linked to Christ by a fisherman's remark that it has been dead for three days. Moreover, as marvelous apparition, the fish replaces the statue of Christ from the opening moments. The fact that this "Icythus" will not rise again becomes another—and conclusive—denial of regeneration for Marcello and his society.

Throughout the sequence, Marcello remains numb. He does not share in the astonishment (the last, diminished, sign of idealization) generated among his companions by the beached monster. When he is confronted by the potentially revitalizing image and voice of Paola, his intelligence is so deadened that he can neither recognize nor identify her. He lacks even the minimal, mechanical, powers of mind he still possessed at the bus stop with Anna Steiner. In her presence he remains, like the fish, heavy and tied to the earth. He slumps to a sitting position in the sand, he can rise only to his knees when Paola gets his attention, then he sinks back on his heels as his attempts to understand her fail. He remains leaden even as he is dragged away from Paola by Lisa. Unlike Zampanò and Augusto he is still able to move, yet his movement is a mere imitation of life—no less tragic and spiritless than their concluding stasis.

In terms of Marcello, the annulment process is pretty much finished when the party is over. His experience (more precisely, his inability to experience) at the beach merely confirms the state of depletion reached by the end of the party. In terms of the film as a whole, however, the annulment is complete only when Marcello and his companions exit. Like Augusto's death and Oscar's escape into the woods, the disappearance of Marcello's society from the world of the film cancels out all that has gotten in the way of creative life. His end becomes a beginning, as Paola takes over and heralds new possibilities.

Paola's name makes her a feminine incarnation of St. Paul, the most profound and influential of early Christian theologians. (Fellini will again refer to Paul in 8½ when a priest suggests to Guido that the hero of his film is undergoing a "journey to Damascus.") Though Paul's writings have been used to support the more repressive and dualistic aspects of Christian orthodoxy, they also contain the seeds of an evolutionary theology similar to Fellini's. They emphasize the need for transformation from physical existence to spiritual life—and from a life ruled by the law (convention, authority) to a life of liberation through love.

In a sense, in the final moments Paola enacts the transformations spoken of by Paul, as she undergoes a visual process similar to Cabiria's at the end of her film. Initially, she is tied to the "world's body"—shot from a distance in full length, located three-dimensionally in space, visibly rooted to the earth. Mentally, she is tied to the past as she tries to repossess Marcello through pantomime reminders of their prior meeting. However, when Marcello cannot respond she is released from his world of givenness and physical appropriation. Instead of trying to capture his attention, she waves good-bye. At the same time, her image becomes etherealized as she is shot in increasing closeup. Her feet and lower body disappear and so, finally, does all but her head—freeing her entirely from earth. The physical environment behind and around her metamorphoses from images of specific objects to shades and forms of light. Three-dimensionality gives way to two-dimensionality as objects separated in space give way to a single, unified plane in which an enlightened Paola and her light-environment are one. The locus of Paola's activity then shifts from her hand to her eye—the organ for touching the world not as matter but as image and spirit.

The moment Marcello disappears, she—like Cabiria—miraculously discovers the camera eye and the eyes and souls of the viewers. She can now establish an eye-to-eye, soul-to-soul relation with the unseen but present. She has joined Cabiria in the realm of fully spiritualized experience.

The Camera Eye as Creative Spirit

The miraculous emergence of affirmation from annulment is not only the result of the kind of "creative negation" we have noted in discussing the end of *Il Bidone*, it is also rooted in a distinction clearly at work in *La Dolce Vita* between the imaginative envisionment and the mere living out of tragedy. Unlike Marcello, who is so caught up in annulment that he becomes its victim, the camera eye can see annulment as a liberating possibility—the means of negating tragic limitation. More than that, it can affirm the necessity of annulment in a world that must pass away before new life can evolve. (As Fellini has said: "I feel that decadence is indispensable to rebirth.")[5]

The creative function of the camera eye in *La Dolce Vita* culminates a subtle development through Fellini's early films. From *Variety Lights* through "A Matrimonial Agency," the camera remains trapped in the world it has witnessed. However, at the end of *La Strada*, it pulls up and away from Zampanò, and though it fails to free itself entirely, it begins to take on a life of its own. At the end of *Il Bidone*, this becomes even more pronounced, as the camera leaves the dead Augusto behind and witnesses, from a distance, the community that embodies everything Augusto lacks. In each case, independence takes the form of escape. However, at the end of *The Nights of Cabiria*, the camera achieves autonomy through integration, not escape, as tragedy is replaced by affirmation. When Cabiria discovers the camera eye, it loses its conventional invisibility as a mere spectator-recorder. It acquires a vital invisibility, a nonvisible presence, that makes it equal in importance to Cabiria herself.

In *La Dolce Vita*, the camera is again freed from tragedy and again becomes vitally present through Paola's acknowledgment of it. In addition, the camera acquires a whole new dimension of creative life. For one thing, it depends much less on its main character than it did in preceding Fellini films. Sequences begin and end without Marcello, and even in the middle of scenes, the camera abandons him to witness activities which strike it as more interesting and relevant. As this might suggest, the camera enjoys highly privileged perception. It attends Marianne's crucial discussion of true religious experience. It sees characters such as Sylvia, Fanny, and, of course, Marcello, in ways that no one in the film can. Finally, and most important, it comes to see Paola with a clarity that Marcello cannot even approach. (The camera's extraordinary vision is accentuated by Fellini's use of cinemascope and by the unprecedented aerial photography of the opening sequence—before the camera chooses to descend into Marcello's restricted world of annulment.)

Coupled with its independent and privileged vision are attributes that a camera eye always tends to have but that Fellini turns into a major spiritual and aesthetic fact in *La Dolce Vita*. The camera eye is everywhere, yet nowhere. It sees all in its world, but has no visible, physical form. Strictly speaking, there is no "camera," no "eye"—only the process that we see unfolding on screen. (I will, however, retain the term "camera eye" for simplicity's sake, rather than use a term such as "envisioning power" which, though more accurate, would quickly turn into jargon.) Moreover, the power of unfolding involves not just seeing but creating, organizing, communicating—for the camera eye serves as the source of the work of art before our eyes. Since there is no physical, external, source, this power is entirely immanent. Since it is what it shows and does, it is manifest as pure act, pure creation.

Finally—and quite crucial to the context of *La Dolce Vita*—this power, though immanent, is unacknowledged by its world. On numerous occasions, Fellini violates convention and has his characters look directly at the camera. In some cases, they respond only with a dead stare (like Federica at the beginning of the Castle sequence). In other instances, when the camera has adopted Marcello's point of view, characters respond only to Marcello. Jane does this when she looks right at the camera but says "You're crazy" to Marcello. The most striking example occurs at the beginning of Steiner's party. When Anna comes out to greet Marcello (and Emma), Marcello is invisible, and Anna appears to be greeting the camera and inviting it into the apartment. Then Steiner appears to be addressing it when he rises and first approaches. But as he gets closer, his gaze subtly

A new vision of the angelic and spiritual dominates the final moments as a "grounded" Marcello and his society of exhausted revellers are annulled.

shifts screen left, Marcello suddenly pops into sight, screen left, and we discover that Steiner has been seeing Marcello all along. In effect, the Steiners have been blind to the creative source of life in their world, and Marcello, in turn, has acted as a barrier between them and that source.

As an all-envisioning power that is omnipresent yet invisible, manifest as pure creative act, present yet unacknowledged by Marcello's world, the camera eye becomes a model of nothing less than the Creative or "Divine" Power itself. Divinity in this respect is not a personal God or Author of the universe but the miracle of life's self-creation—the miracle of life "narrating" itself. Since this power is identified with the spectator (we "envision" the film at the same time the camera eye does, and when characters look at the camera they are also looking at us), *we* are elevated by the film experience into divine narrators of life.

Once we see that the role of the camera eye has been transformed by Fellini into that of Creative Spirit, the end of the film becomes even clearer, even more profound. The life of the spirit, living in a world that has become inured to it, must witness to the annulment of that world. Through Marcello that process is accomplished, and through the final appearance of Paola the life of the spirit is finally reaffirmed. Her face, eyes, and smile confirm that the world can now not only acknowledge but radiate spirit. The divine power is now indwelling. A Second Coming has, indeed, been fulfilled.

10

Summing Up: Fellini's Development Through *La Dolce Vita*

I have chosen *La Dolce Vita* as the feature film to conclude my study of Fellini's early work for two reasons. First of all, the feature following *La Dolce Vita*—8½—is a radical departure in terms of style and technique. It marks an entirely new kind of filmmaking and introduces a decade of films (1963–72, 8½ through *Roma*) in which Fellini focuses on processes of imaginative liberation without the negativity that characterizes all the early films except *The Nights of Cabiria*. Moreover, *La Dolce Vita* serves to culminate and "summarize" a coherent phase of development from *Variety Lights* through *The Nights of Cabiria* in which the possibility for creative life slowly evolves and finally flourishes.[1]

Variety Lights to *The Nights of Cabiria*

As the preceding chapters seek to imply, the progression toward creative experience in Fellini's early work is expressed principally through the development of consciousness within his main characters. The characters of the first two films—*Variety Lights* and *The White Sheik*—are so bound to convention and so reliant on illusions handed them by others, that they possess little or nothing in the way of unique conscious life. As we have indicated, the failure of intelligence is reflected in the fact that Checco in *Variety Lights* and Ivan in *The White Sheik* lose consciousness at crucial moments in their story. It is also reflected in the "sick head" syndrome which culminates when Ivan and Wanda end up at an insane asylum near the end of *The White Sheik*. The first real advance toward awakening and awareness occurs in *I Vitelloni* where Moraldo, instead of being absorbed by his conventional world, takes a critical stance toward it. His judgmental attitude hints at a desire for a self-determining existence. Moreover, his rejection of his past, his home town, his friends might—under better circumstances—reflect emergent self-awareness. In fact, this is precisely the kind of negative act upon which self-consciousness is built:

To become conscious of oneself, to be conscious at all, begins with saying 'no.' . . .
And when we scrutinize the acts upon which consciousness and the ego are built

Fellini plays at being an extra during the filming of The Nights of Cabiria.

101

up, we must admit that to begin with they are all negative acts. To discriminate, to distinguish, to mark off, to isolate oneself from the surrounding context—these are the basic acts of consciousness.[2]

Though Moraldo's act of rejection does not work for him (he ends up defeated by negation) it introduces into the Fellini canon a model of behavior that will work when Cabiria is able to renounce prostitution, home, and past in order to die and be reborn as a free and integral being. (Moraldo's act also starts Fellini on the road to the kind of "creative negation" discussed earlier.)

"A Matrimonial Agency" marks the next major advance. As a reporter, the main character proves far more verbal and intellectual than Fellini's preceding heroes. He is also the film's narrator who, by retelling his story, is engaged in highly conscious, reflective activity. Finally—and most important—his intent clearly is to tell a story of growth to awareness through his encounter with Rosanna.

Though the reporter's story proves ironic, as he substitutes the illusion of self-awareness for the real thing, "A Matrimonial Agency" marks the first time that intellectual activity and self-consciousness become the principal concerns within a Fellini film. This leads immediately to *La Strada* in which Gelsomina becomes the first Fellini figure to experience genuine awakening. Moreover, as earlier discussion indicated, *La Strada* is, in a far more profound and comprehensive way than "A Matrimonial Agency," a story of consciousness—focusing as it does on the tragic consequences of a world in which creative intelligence is born, suppressed, projected, then destroyed.

By the time we get to *Il Bidone*, Fellini's subject is no longer the birth and partial development of consciousness but the suppression of a consciousness that is fully and painfully alive. Augusto's constant brooding and depression bespeak an intensity of awareness lacking to preceding Fellini characters. His sullen exterior and his refusal to communicate bespeak an equally intense effort not to confront the alienated consciousness burning within him. In fact, through both his awareness and his refusal to acknowledge it, he becomes the most complicated of Fellini's characters to this point, as well as the most resourceful: forever adopting new strategies to evade self-knowledge. (Augusto's genius at concealment is a principal reason that *Il Bidone* was poorly received by both critics and public. He seemed so inaccessible to viewers that they found little to identify with.) With the appearance of Augusto and *Il Bidone*, the central problem within the Fellini story becomes not the absence or falsification of consciousness but the challenge of transforming it into a liberating rather than a merely alienating force.

The challenge is met in *The Nights of Cabiria*. The heroine embodies Moraldo's capacity for renunciation as well as the urge for maturity that

the reporter thinks he displays in "A Matrimonial Agency." She also possesses Gelsomina's ability for genuine awakening and Augusto's intensity—in addition to her own unique and creative imagination.

The growth toward full consciousness is, quite obviously, a growth in
individuality. The first major advance occurs when the convention-bound
figures of *Variety Lights* and *The White Sheik* give way to Moraldo. As the
first Fellini loner, he ushers in a period of alienated individualism, where
characters are rootless and isolated. Following Moraldo, who never gets
completely free of his town, we have the reporter of "A Matrimonial
Agency," who is completely uprooted from his past and alone in Rome.
(He does, however, remain ensconced in a conventional job in the institutional Roman world.) He is followed by the itinerant heroes of *La
Strada*, attached neither to family nor fixed home. whose occupation puts
them on the margins of society. With Augusto, we get the biggest loner of
all who, as a criminal, is not only marginal but an outcast. (As Fellini's
figures become more alienated, they begin spending time in jail: Zampanò
a day or so, Augusto a much more extended period.) By this point, the
process of "negative individualization" has gone as far as it can go. The only
alternative other than repetition of the same kind of story and character is
Cabiria's story: reintegration of the alienated individual with the world he/
she has left behind.

Interestingly, the progression of Fellini's characters—in terms of both
consciousness and individuality—provides a near classic case of ego differentiation and personality development, as they would be described by
Jung and his followers. Fellini's heroes (mirroring the ego) gradually break
free of the "wombed" world of unconscious existence. They seek increasing autonomy, defining themselves in opposition to that world and reaching a state of extreme polarity. Following this is the leap to individuation
in which the polarity between ego and other is dissolved, and wholeness
is attained. Fellini, of course, was not working any of this out intentionally;
it is merely an unconscious reflection of his own imaginative development. It is no wonder, though, given the correlation of Fellini's vision with
Jung's views of individuation, that Fellini came to be an ardent student of
the noted psychologist.

The development of consciousness through Fellini's early films is associated with a growing emphasis on possibility as opposed to mere givenness. Part of what makes Moraldo's actions at the end of *I Vitelloni* so
significant is that they are the first major indication that a Fellini character
senses something missing. A sense of possibility is forcefully articulated
for the very first time (albeit inauthentically) in "A Matrimonial Agency,"
when the reporter-narrator talks of the "countless possibilities life presents each day." Following this, *La Strada* becomes the first Fellini film to
give real preeminence to possibility. It introduces, at the very beginning,
the potential for wholeness offered by Gelsomina, and the film's tragedy

lies in the failure of such potential to become actual (i.e., in the continued and increasingly irreversible *absence* of wholeness). Moreover, from the moment he buys Gelsomina to replace the dead Rosa to his final devastation, Zampanò is moved principally by things missing. At the same time, Gelsomina is the first Fellini character who genuinely tries to change—sensing the need to become entirely different from what she initially is.

With *Il Bidone*, we have a story conceived even more fully in terms of absence. The opening swindle hinges on something buried. Augusto sublimates everything of value, then becomes obsessed with a sense of something missing and a need to change his life. The subsidiary characters (until Susanna accepts her role as "suffering saint" at the end) are also obsessed with change. Roberto wants to become a singer; Picasso dreams of being a successful painter; Iris desires a far different relationship with Picasso.

This all leads to *The Nights of Cabiria* where, as we have demonstrated, the heroine's imaginative development is directly the result of an ability to intuit what is missing and possible, to see beyond the seen, and finally to reach a stage of spiritual fulfillment characterized by the miraculous presentness of absence.

As possibility replaces mere givenness, the nature of illusion changes. The paltry dreams of Fellini's early characters are all false attempts to deny a given reality, because they are derived from that reality. For example, the White Sheik is just as much a given for Wanda as is Ivan—even if the givenness lies in cartoons. In trying to escape Ivan's mundane world for the Sheik's presumably exotic one, Wanda is merely substituting one kind of external reality for another. Because this kind of illusion is not self-created, it does not answer to the needs of the characters who embrace it: it merely leads to loss of identity. In contrast, the illusions Cabiria embraces always correlate precisely with what she needs in order to grow. She may entertain fantasies of happiness ever after through marriage, but they emerge from a profound desire for love. More important, she is able to transform conventional fantasies into means of personal fulfillment so that something like "marriage" becomes not a mere social or religious institution but a fully realized metaphor for involvement and integration.

The increase in creative capability on the part of Fellini's characters is accompanied by a growing emphasis on redemption and resurrection. Implicit in both is a sense that the past is not inalterably given, that it can be re-created and ultimately transcended by acts of imagination. We have dealt with this at some length in *Il Bidone* and *The Nights of Cabiria*, but redemption and resurrection surface in significant ways earlier in Fellini's career. In *I Vitelloni*, the possibility of redemption is introduced through the narrative device of voice-over. Speaking in the past tense, the narrator has a sense of history—as well as the opportunity to reformulate it, make it anew. However, he makes no effort to do so. He seeks only to recount it. Such is not the case for the narrator-reporter of "A Matrimonial Agency." It becomes clear as he retells *his* story that he is reorganizing the events he experienced into a tale of moral awakening. Moreover, as a character in the past who is now narrator he has, in effect, undergone a death and rebirth.

With *La Strada*, resurrection and redemption become insistent motivating forces in the lives of the characters. Zampanò's attempt to replace the dead Rosa with her sister clearly emerges from a wish to resurrect Rosa, and it makes his relation with Gelsomina an attempt to redeem the past. Gelsomina (who is repeatedly visualized undergoing death and rebirth) shows an even greater talent for resurrecting things. When Zampanò fails her as a companion, she reinvents him (with *Il matto's* help) as an abstraction (a potential husband and purpose for living). When she and *Il matto* are separated, she resurrects *him* through his song. Resurrection is so prominent that it actually becomes the final killing force. It is in response to the young woman's re-creation of Gelsomina (in memory and song) that Zampanò ends the film in a state of collapse.

As Fellini's films move toward a redemptive view of life, patterns of experience evolve from the merely linear to the circular, semicircular, "helical." His initial films place great emphasis on railway imagery. In *Variety Lights*, Checco and Liliana first meet on board a train, and they end the film entrained to different destinations. *The White Sheik* begins with Ivan and Wanda arriving by rail in Rome and ends with the two of them as part of a "train" or procession of Ivan's relatives, chugging all in a line to St. Peter's. (The train is clearly precursor to all the parade and procession imagery of later Fellini films.) In *I Vitelloni*, Moraldo ends up in a railway compartment as Guido is stop-framed on the tracks. The rigid linearity of the railroad gives way to the somewhat greater flexibility of the road in Fellini's next three films. The narrator of "A Matrimonial Agency" enjoys the freedom of an automobile, yet he ends his story in much the same way as prior Fellini figures—traveling in a straight line, screen center, away from the camera eye. Zampanò's motor home and the various cars in which Augusto rides provide greater options for travel and experience in the two films following "A Matrimonial Agency." Moreover, in *La Strada*, the linear thrust of the road is balanced by circularity. Zampanò's principal act involves wrapping himself in a chain. He always moves in a circle as he describes his act to the audience. And much of his time (as well as that of the other characters) is spent in a circus. In *Il Bidone*, circularity lies less in specific imagery than in the sense of a past tragically repeating itself. (Augusto lives out the words of a dead man's letter; Patrizia's appearance resurrects a dead personal past; Augusto is driven at the end to repeat the farm swindle from the beginning.)

The line and the circle are both, obviously, expressions of a limited world. The line allows for motion and forward thrust, but only in a regimented, predetermined way. The circle allows for a kind of wholeness—but wholeness born of closure, exclusion, repetition, and, ultimately, stasis. The "solution" is a spiral or curvilinear process that moves both forward and back, that sweeps wide and far as it progresses and recapitulates. The spiral becomes a model of dynamic wholeness, of encompassing thrust. This model is first suggested at the end of *Il Bidone* through the community of women and children weaving among each other and moving around a bend. It is also suggested at the end of *The Nights of Cabiria* as the heroine's co-celebrants complement her forward motion with their swirling circles—and as her ever scanning eyes trace arcs of experience that embrace even the unseen. The model presented below—

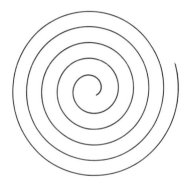

a (concentric) spiral—comes to characterize the nature of Cabiria's experiences as she continually recapitulates her past in a way that makes her present richer, more integral. (Her initial near-drowning is, as we have noted, recapitulated through the shipwreck fantasy at the Lux and through cliffside death and rebirth at the end. In addition, her romantic encounter with the movie star Lazzari becomes her love relationship with the consummate role-player Oscar, and her pilgrimage experience is reincarnated in the appearance of Brother Giovanni. The entire film is structured in terms of "creative repetition.")

As the concentric spiral is intended to suggest, Cabiria is able to expand outward without ever losing her center, in ever-widening arcs and cycles of adventure, recapitulation, redemption, and further adventure. She moves backward only to move forward, and vice versa, encompassing an ever-greater range of experience and keeping always on the move. As we have already seen, this method of experience becomes transpersonal. The creative "othering" of perpetual expansion moves her beyond limiting personal identity and physical death, and puts her in touch with the universal sources of transformation, fulfilling the goal of religious experience and the possibility for a resurrection beyond death.

As Fellini's story and characters evolve through the early films, so does his narrative method. Most noticeable is the diminishment in plot or conventional story line and the emergence, instead, of a more complex kind of narrative structure. *Variety Lights* and *The White Sheik* are traditional and linear in development; a summary of their plots even seems to serve as a summary of the films. It takes a certain amount of effort to see beyond the literal to something of greater significance. *I Vitelloni*, composed as it is of multiple stories, is much less conventional. However, each story is itself plotted, and effort is still required to see beyond the plot to something greater. With "A Matrimonial Agency" and *La Strada*, we move from realistic story to narratives conceived principally in imaginative terms. Particularly with *La Strada*, it becomes obvious that the film is structured as a spiritual and psychological tale to which plot, per se, is secondary.

The secondary nature of the plot is even clearer by the time we get beyond *Il Bidone* to *The Nights of Cabiria*. Cabiria's escapades seem random and disconnected unless they are seen as part of her growth to enlightenment. Moreover, the final scene explodes plot altogether. The appearance of the adolescents and the "happy ending" they provide make no sense in literal terms but are perfectly apropos within the imaginative context of Cabiria's spiritualization. Even more unrealistic is Cabiria's wholly unexpected glance at the camera eye and us.

Ever since Fellini left realism and conventional structure behind, he has been subject to attack as undisciplined, self-indulgent, irrational, unintelligible. There are many filmgoers (and many critics among them) who much prefer Fellini's earlier movies. Yet his later films are no less coherent or unified; they are merely organized in a different and more complex way.

Fellini's abandonment of plot is closely linked to the growing autonomy of his characters, the growing emphasis on possibility over necessity. Plot, as writers from Aristotle to E. M. Forster have suggested, is principally a causal mechanism. One thing gives rise to another which (inevitably) gives rise to a third, and so on. It is no accident that Aristotle "discovered" plot in Greek tragedy—and, especially, in *Oedipus Rex*—where individual freedom proves illusory in the face of an external moral order. And even up to the twentieth century, plot continued to be the literary reflection of a worldview that affirmed first causes and a fixed order of things (divine providence, the great chain of being, the divine right of kings, a social contract, and so on).

In this context, it is only appropriate that characters such as Ivan and Checco, Fausto and Alberto—all of whom long for security within an established order—inhabit a densely plotted fictional universe. It is equally appropriate that once characters begin to become self-causing, conventional story line begins to diminish. Accordingly, it is Moraldo, the first Fellini character to renounce his conventional world, who first fractures plot when he abruptly exits town at the end of *I Vitelloni*. His action is "discontinuous," unprepared for. It is the kind of sudden leap that Cabiria experiences in a much more fulfilling way when she transcends plot at the conclusion of her story.

As the organizational nature of Fellini's films changes, so does the nature of characterization. Fellini's earliest figures—particularly Ivan, Wanda, Checco, and the White Sheik—are mere caricatures. (The fact that *The White Sheik* is named after a comic strip hero accentuates the stereotyping in that particular film.) Later figures such as Fausto, Alberto, Moraldo, Zampanò, and Augusto are fully realized, "rounded" characters. They give the impression of being "real people"—which is what traditional drama strives to create. However, Gelsomina and *Il matto* introduce a kind of portrayal other than caricature or dramatic characterization. Consistent with the fact that they are part of an imaginative, spiritual, tale, they are "envisioned powers," embodiments of certain spiritual possibilities. For instance, Gelsomina acquires coherence not from the fact that she brings a stock set of responses to every situation (as a stereotype would). Nor does she derive it from acting like a "real person" (how many Gelsominas exist in the day-to-day world!). She gains it almost entirely from the potential she holds for consciousness, wholeness, and so forth. She is the *spirit* of growth, the *spirit* of possibility and aspiration; that is her unique and compelling narrative identity. This is even more the case with Cabiria. (Again, surely, no one has encountered a Cabiria—much less a *prostitute* like Cabiria—in the real world.)

In a sense, the above distinction is fully validated only through later Fellini figures: Juliet (*of the Spirits*), Toby Dammit, Encolpio, and the various personae (actor, director, narrative eye and imagination, voice-over narrator) that Fellini himself adopts in his first-person films (*Fellini: A Director's Notebook*, *The Clowns*, and *Roma*.) Through them it becomes obvious that Fellini is out to create not traditional characters but vehicles for the examination of various imaginative possibilities. With Gelsomina and Cabiria, Fellini is still working in partially dramatic terms, and there remains much of dramatic characterization within each.

By fashioning his human figures in increasingly imaginative terms, Fellini is not becoming allegorical or abstract. He is not creating one level of action merely to refer to something beyond it. Gelsomina and Cabiria do not stand for wholeness or possibility, they embody it concretely in their actions and relationships. And the stories of *La Strada* and *Cabiria* do not symbolize (in the restrictive sense) the struggle for growth, they *are* such struggles. The fact that these stories are spiritual in nature does not make them any less "real," direct, specific, or intrinsically valid.

Similarly, the fact that later Fellini figures are powers more than realistic characters does not mean that they are dehumanized. In fact, because they tend to be the embodiments of *ideally* human powers, they are consummately human, suprahuman. However—and this is where some viewers tend to have trouble with later Fellini figures—the less dramatically realistic they become, the less readily we can identify with them either as "people" or (as is more often the case with viewer-identification) as reflections of ourselves. We must, instead, make an imaginative leap and see them not in terms of what we are but in terms of what we might be. We must live beyond the limits of our own fixed character and identity and be open for the same kind of redemptive self-creation that Fellini's figures undergo.

We have not, up till now, dwelt specifically on the "filmic" dimension of Fellini's films. The principal reason is that, despite the changes we have noted in plot and characterization, the style of his early films tends to remain more dramatic than cinematic. By and large, Fellini spent the first phase of his career schooling himself in the basics of the medium. It is only with "The Temptations of Dr. Antonio" and *8½* that he begins to experiment radically with film form and to make the nature and aesthetics of cinema the principal subject of his work.

Consistent with this, the camera eye, particularly in his films prior to *The Nights of Cabiria,* tends to function principally as a photographic mechanism, replicating the external world. Like his early characters, it is at the mercy of what is there. To the extent that there is a discernible style in Fellini's early work, it lies more in what is placed in front of the camera than in "camera creativity" or in a significant relationship between camera and world.

Of course, the early films do provide hints of the visual intensity and originality that characterize Fellini's later work. As early as the opening scene of *The White Sheik* (the first film over which Fellini had full directorial control), we encounter a truly cinematic universe. As Ivan and Wanda disembark in Rome, the camera movement, the activity of people and objects on screen, and the rapid-fire editing create a world which could only be rendered through movies. The same is true during the shooting of the *White Sheik* comic strip. But, much as the live action is turned into still photos for the *White Sheik fumetto*, the visual dynamic of Ivan's and Wanda's world is ultimately sacrificed as they succumb to the devitalizing authority of bourgeois family and church. With *I Vitelloni*, Fellini introduces a kind of fluidness and transparency that will later serve to express the spiritual lightness of experience. He achieves this through the frequent coupling of a moving camera with dissolves. The most resonant cinematic moment in light of Fellini's later work is the late night walk of Leopoldo and Natale from a café to the beach. The powerful sounds and gusts of wind; the flickering, shadowing lights; the unsettling soundtrack music; the swirling movement of characters and objects; and the shifting perspectives of the camera—all conspire to create the kind of filmic mystery and magic that will, in a much less ominous way, inform the "Asa Nisi Masa" sequence in *8½*, the early morning fog sequence in *Amarcord*, and numerous other moments in recent Fellini work.

La Strada, in addition to presenting the same kind of visual and aural magic in the brief Oswaldo scene, offers the most fully realized cinematic moment in Fellini's films prior to *The Nights of Cabiria*: the transition from country to town during Gelsomina's short-lived abandonment of Zampanò. The shift in lighting (bright to gloomy), in music (airy to ponderous), in space (open to closed), in human image (from few and free to many and trapped)—as well as the use of camera placement and dissolves to emphasize Gelsomina's sudden absorption and subordination—convey in totally cinematic terms not only the facts but the implications of what is going on. Fellini here makes full use of the medium instead of relying principally on one aspect, or on literary or dramatic means.

Il Bidone, perhaps because it was shot in such a short period of time, does not offer any purely cinematic moments such as this—though it demonstrates Fellini's growing commitment to seeing and filming a world on the move. (In many ways, the automobile is a major "character.") The real breakthrough occurs with *The Nights of Cabiria*. In the scene of Cabiria's drowning and resuscitation, Fellini reveals a greater willingness than ever before to replace the spatial and temporal continuity of dramatic perspective (i.e., the viewpoint of a spectator watching a play on a stage) with multiple, discontinuous, cinematic space and time created through the use of varied camera placements and frequent cuts. This kind of multiple perspective is also evident in other scenes of heightened activity or emotion, such as the pilgrimage and Cabiria's cliffside confrontation with Oscar.

In addition, Fellini repeatedly strives for visual expression that has the lightness of cinema rather than the solidity of physical life—or of theater. (Theater, as has often been noted, is distinguished from cinema by the physical presence of its performers.) There is no attempt to preserve the three-dimensionality of human figures—their status as "real people" being photographed. Emphatic camera movement (tracking shots, pans, tilts) coupled with shots from the waist (or higher) up creates the sense of images floating in a noncorporeal universe. The use of more dissolves than in preceding films heightens the sense of airiness and insubstantiality. And, of course, the dynamism, quickness, and smallness of Cabiria contribute to the feeling that her world is beyond the gravity and weight of material existence.

By far the most important development in specifically cinematic terms is the active role taken by the camera. No longer is style principally what happens in front of the camera; it is created by the camera through its relationship to what it sees. Even at its most passive, the camera communicates a sense of "thereness" or purposeful omnipresence not evident in earlier films. It does so through a combination of infrequent long shots with frequent intimate (though not necessarily closeup) shots. By using both, Fellini gives the camera its multiperspectival quality. However, he uses long shots so infrequently that they do not emphasize the camera's capacity for distanced vision—nor do they suggest a predisposition toward it. Quite the contrary. They establish a distanced view as an option which the camera eye prefers to forego in favor of working "on the inside." The sense of intimacy is further accentuated by the slightly low-angle position the camera tends to take in relation to characters—placing it clearly *in* their world. (The beginning of the pilgrimage sequence offers a good example of the camera "mingling" with its subjects.)

Not only is the camera there and on the inside, it moves with the world it sees, following characters or events in a manner that conveys active interest in what is happening. Very often, it will initiate its activity with a pan, suggesting a search for something worth focusing on. Once the search is rewarded, it will track or resume panning in order to keep its attention squarely on the object of curiosity.

This sense of visual engagement is enhanced by the activity of the heroine herself. As we have suggested earlier, Cabiria is, above all else, a creature of vision. She lives with her eyes and looks with utter intensity, even when she is trying to see beyond the seen. Not only does she see the world, she sees the world seeing her—and that two-way dynamic becomes a means of dissolving the self-world dichotomy that exists early in the film. In short, Cabiria makes vision the subject of her story, and— particularly when she looks at the camera eye and us—she makes the attainment of wholeness synonymous with enlightened vision. Confronted with such a vital, involved visualist, then with a camera eye that is always on the move or placing itself at the center of things, we are compelled to invest the latter with all Cabiria's passion to see. We have no choice but to respond to the workings of the camera eye as far more than the mere mechanical recording of a preexisting reality.

La Dolce Vita

Following upon *The Nights of Cabiria, La Dolce Vita* serves as the summation of the first major phase of Fellini's career. It includes both the tragic dimension of the early films in Marcello's story and the affirmative aspects of *Cabiria* in the relation between Paola and the camera eye. In fact, almost everything of significance from the preceding films reappears in *La Dolce Vita*. The failure to reach any level of awareness (*Variety Lights, The White Sheik, I Vitelloni*) recurs in the episode with Marcello's father, who cannot get beyond immediate and illusory forms of self-gratification. This, as we have noted, is Fellini's "provincial story"—connected with the small-town mentality of figures like Checco, Ivan, Fausto, and Alberto. Much as Checco and Melina end their trip to Rome by boarding a train back to the provinces, Marcello's father ends his en route to the train station and, ultimately, home.

The story of failed and devastating breakout (Moraldo in *I Vitelloni*) is relived by Marcello—as is the story of alienated objectivity ("A Matrimonial Agency"). The development of a consciousness that proves ultimately inadequate (Gelsomina in *La Strada*) is, of course, what Marcello undergoes via Sylvia and Steiner. The denial of consciousness and of self (Augusto in *Il Bidone*) is what Marcello "achieves" in the annulment scenes.

Though the negative dimension of *La Dolce Vita* recalls Fellini's films prior to *The Nights of Cabiria*, it is clear that, having made *Cabiria*, Fellini is not about to restrict himself to the diminished level of human potential displayed in the early films. Indicative of this is the role of awareness among the principal characters. Though Marcello falls victim to externalized consciousness and suffers a fate similar to that of Gelsomina and Augusto, the power of consciousness in Marcello's story is much stronger. This is implicit in the fact that, as a writer with literary aspirations, he is an intellectual—far more so than the reporter in "A Matrimonial Agency." Moreover, two of the characters Marcello meets en route to awakening and disillusionment—Maddalena and Steiner—are far more advanced intellectually than prior Fellini characters. They painfully and articulately acknowledge the conditions of their life. Neither is very successful at suppression or self-evasion. Particularly through Steiner, the problem of self-knowledge is pushed to the point of extreme alienation which it will occupy at the beginning of Guido's struggle for wholeness in 8½.

When we turn to Fellini's narrative method, we again see that *La Dolce Vita* is both a summation and an advance. On the one hand, we have the same sense of limited and diminishing options that characterized the early movies and that was reflected in their heavily "plotted" nature. Yet, conventional plot is even less evident here than in *The Nights of Cabiria.* The film just explodes from scene to scene. Its modernist, discontinuous structure makes it much closer in style to *8½* and subsequent films than to *Cabiria.*

Structural discontinuity is, of course, associated with the freedom of the camera eye: its ability to be anywhere and everywhere, free of the constraints of plot. And it is the camera eye in *La Dolce Vita* which, more than anything else, points beyond *The Nights of Cabiria* and the early films. Fellini's use of the camera provides an entirely new dimension to the story of affirmation that he is in the process of discovering. Moreover, it makes the *nature* of cinema (the camera eye as "character" or power) a crucial subject of Fellini's art. Finally, it moves his imagination to the point where the filmmaking experience will begin to serve as a model of transformation in films such as *8½, The Clowns, Director's Notebook,* and *Roma.*

11

Intermezzo: "The Temptations of Dr. Antonio"

Between *La Dolce Vita* and *8½*, Fellini made "The Temptations of Dr. Antonio" (1962), an episode in a film anthology entitled *Boccaccio '70* (produced by Carlo Ponti, with other episodes directed by Luchino Visconti, Vittorio DeSica, and Mario Monicelli). As our placement of this discussion is intended to emphasize, "Dr. Antonio" is truly a threshold film. Though it is clearly an early film in terms of its negative vision, it is far closer to *8½*, *Juliet of the Spirits*, and other of Fellini's later films in terms of stylistic innovation and filmic method. As a result, our discussion of "Dr. Antonio" will, in a sense, allow us a sneak preview of the future.

Much like *La Dolce Vita*, "The Temptations of Dr. Antonio" begins with a god of Love. Here, instead of a statue of Christ, we have an androgynous Eros who speaks in a little girl's voice but refers to himself as a god (not goddess) and identifies himself as the traditionally male Greek love deity. He also establishes himself as the narrative or creative source of all we see, and thus the connection between camera eye and Creative Spirit, which was implicit in *La Dolce Vita*, becomes explicit. However, there are significant differences between Eros and "Christ," which point to a difference in focus between the two films. The statue represented a decadent Christianity in which spirit had been replaced by institutions, symbols, external material forms. Eros, in contrast, is of an earlier age—before the rigidifying effects of Christian civilization. (Fellini will return to this age, in much greater detail, with *Satyricon*.) Accordingly, Eros is dynamic, not rigid. He is alive, bubbling over with good feeling, narratively omnipresent, attracted to scenes of vitality, motion, and fun. Perhaps most important, he is actively trying to better the human condition ("if I didn't make such an effort to give happiness to people, it would be a catastrophe").[1] He represents the natural outpouring of creative, engaged life—of "love" in the fullest sense. And, as narrator/creator, he is initially able to fulfill the role he possessed at his apogee in Greek myth: the binding force of all things.

Unfortunately, though he is not *of* the world represented by Christ's statue, Eros is hopelessly trapped *in* it. All around him, spirit has become

Fellini looms over the scale model of the E.U.R. district of Rome, which is "terrorized" by Anita Ekberg in "The Temptations of Dr. Antonio."

compartmentalized and sterile. (The opening shots reveal uniformed face-less nuns, separated from uniformed faceless girls, who in turn are separated from uniformed faceless priests.) Despite his attraction to vital, whole life, he can for the most part only narrate a world that is diametrically opposed to what he embodies. Though he is much more closely related to human affairs than was the statue of Christ, he remains, like the statue, an outsider. As a "god," he is a fictional projection of what is lacking within—and he must act upon men who have lost touch with their own potential divinity. (This is why, as he notes, he must "make such an effort" to create happiness.)

Moreover, the price of involvement in the contemporary world is his own compartmentalization and decline. During the opening sequence he suffers diminishment similar to what he has undergone in mythology, where he has been reduced from a cosmogonic spirit of creation and unity to a mere symbol of love and beauty, then to a petty mischievous child responsible only for inciting physical attraction.[2] Initially, he narrates a world (albeit an institutional one) of spirituality: priests, nuns, and churches. Suggestions of spirituality, however, are rapidly replaced by images of romantic coupling (a warrior rescues and carries off a maiden in distress during the filming of a Roman epic) then by a scene of sexual pursuit (two men in a paddle boat madly chase two women in another boat). The sequence concludes with romantic love attained, sexual pursuit rewarded, as we see two lovers reclining on a hillside.

Unable to narrate true spirit in the institutionalized Roman world, Eros has been forced to adopt romantic love as a substitute. The limitations of such love are evident in the inertia of the hillside couple and, even more so, in their isolation. They are far removed (as is Eros by now) from the city and community at large. As soon as Eros aligns himself with mortal rather than divine love, he becomes subject to the world of mortals and to the kind of inauthentic spirituality that prevails in a world of institutionalized religion. When the hillside lovers appear so does Dr. Antonio, superimposed over them in a photograph. He comes prepared to attack Eros with a repressive Catholic moralism rooted in sexual obsession and alienation. (Antonio is named after the father of monasticism who, after renouncing a social existence, was besieged by numerous sexual "temptations" or visions.)[3] Terrified by love and openness in any form, Antonio copes by reducing love to prurience and opposing it on moral grounds. With Antonio's appearance, Eros is further diminished. Distracted by Antonio's ridiculous moralistic attacks, he stops narrating scenes of romance and begins showing only scenes of Antonio doing battle against sex (in a lovers' lane, at a theater). Moreover, he turns from god of love into god of satiric attack, adopting a sardonic tone toward Antonio and, finally, narrating a black and white silent film comedy which is a blatant parody of Antonio. Having allowed himself to get caught up in Antonio's harshly dualistic world (spirit versus flesh, morality versus sexuality, "Logos" versus "Eros"), Eros has, in effect, canceled himself out—which explains, in part, his sudden disappearance as narrator once the black and white film ends.

As soon as Eros vanishes as voice-over, he is reborn as a mysterious little girl who "incarnates" his voice. However, in reincarnated form, Eros has lost his divinity. As mere character, he has sacrificed his invisibility, transcendence, and narrative powers of creation and unification. He also loses his androgyny. More a part of Antonio's polarized world than ever, he is forced into a single sexual identity which is the opposite of Antonio's.

In addition, the little girl, though a highly promising image at first, proves to be ineffectual. She initially possesses Eros's youthful ebullience, spontaneity, playfulness, and sense of joy. She embodies, in short, what is most alive and "divine" in the world of mortals. However, like the camera eye or Creative Spirit in *La Dolce Vita*, she is in the world but unacknowledged by it—remaining virtually unnoticed by everyone around her.[4]

Instead of acknowledging Eros's vestigial presence, the world creates its own love divinity: Sex Goddess Anita Ekberg. Moreover, with the appearance of Anita, Eros becomes mechanized. His voice, once the narrative breath of creation, becomes a mere tape recording which accompanies the billboard of Ekberg and mindlessly repeats the advertising theme: "Drink More Milk." (As in *La Dolce Vita*, physical forms of replenishment replace the spiritual.)

Within this context, Antonio's obsession with the billboard proves a form of idolatry—a failure to recognize more authentic forms of the feminine, the loving, the vestigially divine. This is made clear when he fails to relate to the little girl who is frolicking near the billboard in two scenes in which he takes his greatest strides toward obsession.

As Anita Ekberg takes over for Eros and for the child, she also suffers decline. Initially, though her image is visible to the world, she herself remains absent, free—enjoying a "divine" capacity for invisibility plus presence, transcendence plus immanence. In addition, as an evocative and provocative image, she is more a creature of imagination than of flesh. However, when she comes to life in Antonio's vision, she sacrifices her divine freedom and becomes completely present, "given." She remains miraculous only in size (spirit or the marvelous is defined solely in terms of mass, as with the fish at the end of *La Dolce Vita*). Moreover, when Antonio's viciousness goads her into undressing, she reduces herself solely to a body. In this most mortal of forms, Antonio/St. George is able to kill her off.

With even man-made divinity abolished, godliness is reduced to costume and playacting. The little girl reappears in the final scene dressed as Cupid—a puerile Roman descendent of Eros. (My distinction between

Eros and Cupid is only partially justified historically, but is, I believe, fully justified in terms of the film.) In this guise, she has little in common with her divine prototype. Moreover, she has little in common with the girl she once was. Gone is her natural urge to celebrate and applaud. Present instead is an obnoxious, mechanical compulsion to insult—as she repeatedly sticks out her tongue and makes bug-eyed faces at the camera and at us. (Her final appearance is the diametric opposite of the concluding appearances of Cabiria and Paola.) Her negative transformation recapitulates Eros's decline from love god to satirist. Love unacknowledged, unfulfilled, and repressed, has become contrariness in every possible respect.

In a society that has compartmentalized and conventionalized experience, invented sex goddesses to supplant genuine love, and given rise to creatures of delusion such as Dr. Antonio (pure public persona, "Logos" divorced from reality), life inevitably turns to fantasy. This process is presented largely through the proliferation of fictional forms: narration, photography, theater, film, advertising, music, hallucination, painting.

The first hint of fictionalization is the appearance of a narrator—and one of mythological origin.[5] Yet Eros is presented as a narrator not of make-believe but of life. He is clearly not telling a story, he is out in the world, envisioning and describing the natural unfolding of events. Moreover, to the extent that fiction is present at this point (fashion photography in progress in front of a church, filmmaking under way on a street corner), it is part of the world rather than an escape from it. Art is concrete activity rather than artifact.

This changes abruptly with the arrival of Antonio. Introduced through two black and white photos superimposed over the hillside lovers, then by an iris out that reveals him in live action, he personifies the substitution of artifice for experience. Within a few moments of his appearance, he goes from a public park ("reality" or the world at large) to the stage of a theater, then to a movie "role" (in the silent film) which is described by Eros as *"one of his outstanding performances"* (my italics).

As Eros's words and its own contrived nature suggest, the silent film marks a major transition from reality to illusion within the larger film. Eros himself has either lost the ability to distinguish between the two or has become a liar. Instead of acknowledging the fictional, parodic nature of the film, he claims that it is a mere recording of events by someone who happened to be there (a "documentary" in effect). The god of concrete reality, natural unfolding, has fallen victim to Antonio's world of falsifications and become an unreliable narrator. This (like his involvement in satire) necessitates his demise and explains why he fails to survive the film within a film.

At the moment of his disappearance, Eros announces, "At this point our *story* begins" (my italics)—a remark which initially seems out of place. (After all, the story of Dr. Antonio has been under way for some time.) However, when we recall that Eros has been a narrator of life rather than fiction, we realize that his words merely confirm the death of the natural and real and assert that, from here on in, everything will have the status merely of "story."

The little girl who replaces Eros at this point also reflects the movement toward illusion. Despite all the positive things that we have noted about her, she is quite artificial. Not only is she born out of a film within a film, but she is all dressed up as a fancy little bourgeois princess. In effect she is a *symbol* of the naturalness and vitality of Eros, rather than their genuine embodiment. She is all Eros can be in Antonio's world of abstraction.

As soon as the "story" begins, the fictionalization process occurs anew. Though Antonio begins by moving out and about in a public world of churches and newsstands, he quickly gravitates to a field outside his apartment—signaling a movement toward home, privacy, subjectivity. Accordingly, he moves into his head and recalls (for his Boy Scout troop) the boyhood incident in which the aunt of a friend undressed in his presence. He is presumably recalling an actual event, yet he grossly distorts what happened so that it can serve as a lesson to the boys on the dangers and indecencies of women. (The fact that he is fictionalizing is suggested when he describes the event as an "episode" and himself as a "protagonist.") With no justification whatsoever, he calls the aunt a "fallen creature" and then refers to the nakedness of a beautiful woman as a "diabolical spectacle." At this moment, women are turned into fantasy, and the billboard of Anita—media projection and make-believe—is virtually born out of Antonio's words.

The billboard comes to function as a "story" within the story, and once it is in place we have yet another process of fictionalization. At first, Antonio treats the poster as a concrete reality. But when he fails to get it removed through political means, he withdraws into his apartment and into verbal attacks which misrepresent the poster and its effect on people. This leads to hallucination—his vision of Anita's hand and the glass of milk in the mirror—which leads to even more violent denunciations and finally to outright attack with ink bottles. By now the poster of Anita has been distorted into a Symbol of Evil—"the Golden Calf of yore," among other things—in Antonio's imagination.

Antonio's ink attack marks the end of his ability to relate to the outside world. The smudged-up billboard is covered over, and Antonio falls prey to his vision of Anita and the billboard (the next "story" within the story). Within his vision, he moves from seeing Anita as relatively real to seeing her solely in abstract, symbolic terms. Moreover, fictionalization becomes so advanced that his vision turns into a "movie" or pure projection which, unlike the earlier pseudodocumentary, loses all ties with reality, all relation to a filmmaker or an act of filmmaking.

This transformation has, to some extent, been prepared for by the shape of the billboard (a perfect replica of the cinemascope screen on which "Dr. Antonio" itself is shown), by the fact that it has its own "soundtrack" (the tape recording of Eros's voice), and by the fact that it was covered, just prior to the vision, in white—turning it into a blank screen awaiting Antonio's projections. The billboard, in short, has been a latent movie all along. When Anita comes to life, she turns the world into a "moving billboard" which is, of course, precisely what a movie is. Not only that, as a "monster" who "threatens" the city of Rome and picks Antonio up in her giant "paw," she turns Antonio's vision into an homage to *King Kong* and the Japanese horror films of the fifties. Antonio himself finally acknowledges that his vision has become a movie when (as Anita begins to undress) he turns to the camera eye and addresses us-as-audience—telling us not to watch and begging us to take the women and children out of the theater!

At this point, Antonio is fictionalized into a mere image on a screen and, worse still, a piece of celluloid. He has even disappeared as the source of his own vision. (If there were still an Antonio dreaming up what we see, the Antonio within the movie would have addressed the camera eye as his own hallucinating imagination, not as an audience in a theater.) Just as Eros the narrator became projected out into (and replaced by) his "story," Antonio the dreamer has been projected wholly into his "movie." Since we now have a movie instead of a vision, all human agency has been replaced by mechanical unfolding and human, psychological, projection has been supplanted by film projection.

There is still one more step to go in Antonio's fictionalization. Even as a celluloid figure, he is able to acknowledge and address the audience—retaining some shred of identity and individuality. This ends when he becomes St. George, an historical figure out of a painting we have seen in his living room. At the same time, his transformation, which brings about the confrontation between "Satan" (Anita) and the Saint, turns his "movie" into simple-minded allegory: the most abstract and artificial form of narrative invention. This completes Fellini's set of fictional "Chinese boxes." We have an allegory based on a painting, within a vision that has turned into a movie, inspired by a billboard within a "story" that has replaced Eros's narration.

Even after the vision is over and the real world returns, Antonio remains fictionalized. Draped over the poster in a comic parody of intercourse, he has become a physical part of Anita's billboard world!

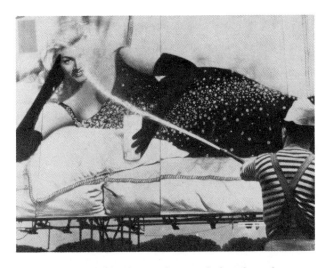

The hosing down of Ekberg's image becomes the launching of a spear as Antonio / St. George loses all touch with reality and attacks the billboard.

Much like *La Strada* and *La Dolce Vita*, "The Temptations of Dr. Antonio" culminates in the destruction of intelligence. The failure of consciousness is implicit in Fellini's choice of Eros as a major narrative device. Even in his days as a cosmogonic power, he was viewed by some as the enemy of reason: "in all gods, in all human beings / [Eros] overpowers the intelligence in the breast, / and all their shrewd planning" (Hesiod).[6] And as he devolved into a mere god of romantic infatuation and physical love, his role as an enemy of rationality and consciousness became all the more pronounced—hence his reduction in sculpture and painting to a child and, even in some instances, to a sleeping infant.

We have already addressed, in other contexts, some of the most crucial aspects of false and failed intelligence—particularly Antonio's growing inability to deal with reality and his consequent insanity. However, it is worth noting how carefully the film is structured in terms of declining consciousness. There are, in effect, five distinct phases: (1) enlightened, unitive consciousness (Eros at his best, out and about, narrating the world); (2) false consciousness gaining control (Antonio, the self-righteous intellectual, bringing about Eros's demise as narrator); (3) the birth and growing power of the unconscious (the appearance of the billboard as a projection of Antonio's repressed sexuality; his growing obsession with Anita); (4) the victory of the unconscious (the billboard comes alive and, through Antonio's hallucinations, takes over for Antonio's conscious life); (5) the death of all consciousness (the killing of Anita, the last incentive for mental life for Antonio, followed by his delirium).

By the final scene, with mind and spirit denied, Antonio is a dead weight—much like Zampanò, Augusto, and Marcello at the end of their stories. He is injected, tied up, lowered from the billboard, carried in a stretcher, dumped into an ambulance. There is only one brief sign of life. Just prior to his disappearance, in response to the mechanical tape recording of Eros's voice, he opens his eyes and weakly wails "Anita." The last flicker of intelligence, it recalls Zampanò's momentary sense of terror and Augusto's delusive "I'm coming with you," before they too relinquished consciousness altogether.

"Dr. Antonio" and Fellini's Later Films

We need not belabor the aspects of "Dr. Antonio" that place it in the company of Fellini's early, "negative" work. Its shared concern with problems of fragmentation, illusion, alienation, false consciousness, and the destruction of love should be obvious. It is much more interesting to see all the ways in which this short but crucial film points to the future.

First of all, though "Dr. Antonio" is not ultimately positive, it is certainly not tragic. There is a comic perspective and an outpouring of comic energy that helps redeem the negativity. This is enhanced by the presence of Eros, whose initial activity offers a model of wholeness and creative life which—though destroyed in the film—remains alive in the viewer's mind as an alternative to all Antonio does. We can laugh freely at Antonio because we know his way is not the only way. This sense of freedom and alternative keeps "Dr. Antonio" from being a "closed" film, and its lack of closure separates it not only from Fellini's tragic movies but from his early comedies (*Variety Lights, The White Sheik*), where neither wholeness nor creativity exists as a real possibility.

Second, despite his many limitations, Dr. Antonio is far more complex and "heady" than any of Fellini's earlier heroes (even Cabiria). As a "visionary," he is clearly kin to his immediate successors, Guido and Juliet, and he pushes Fellini to the brink of an art rooted in creative (rather than repressive) hallucination. (Fellini's use of myth for the first time as his point of departure is indication of his increasingly direct concern with creative thought and the workings of the imagination.)

Third, the film is an outright repudiation of the lingering realism that continued to characterize Fellini's work even through *La Dolce Vita*. The opening sequence of "Dr. Antonio" is like nothing we have seen before in Fellini: an explosion of seemingly unrelated images, locales, and individuals, fracturing the traditional unities of space, time, and action. (The opening scene of *La Dolce Vita*, as bold as it was, still observed the three unities.) Here for the first time, in fully realized form, is the discontinuous, nonlinear, and seemingly nonnarrative progression[7] that have become synonymous with Fellini's later work.

Though the appearance of the ultraconventional Antonio and the disappearance of Eros's divine creative power notably diminish stylistic innovation (entirely apropos "aesthetically"), the film never reverts to the realistic level of Fellini's prior work. Moreover, Antonio himself is responsible for yet another major stylistic development: the movement to a completely invented reality in front of the camera. Though Fellini had used sets before (in fact reconstructed the Via Veneto in shooting *La Dolce Vita*), the effect was principally realistic. Such is definitely not the case with Antonio's sci-fi/horror vision of Anita Ekberg looming over the E.U.R. district, followed by the eerie procession of Antonio's former associates that concludes the vision.[8] The pure fantasy that prevails here is precursor to the marvelously fabricated worlds Fellini will conjure up in films like *Juliet of the Spirits, Satyricon*, and *Casanova*.

Fourth, "Dr. Antonio" is the first film in which Fellini (at least in one instance) supplants characterization completely with imaged "powers" or "spirits"—human images which function not as people but as creative possibilities. The replacement of Eros with the little girl, who is given no dramatic persona, and is merely there as a cinematic image, prefigures the appearance of images such as the woman in white (Claudia Cardinale) in $8\frac{1}{2}$, Juliet's myriad "spirits," and all the dramatically undefined creatures of *Satyricon*. (Interestingly, Fellini was tempted toward this "apparitional" mode in *La Dolce Vita*, as Paola's final appearance makes clear. There, however, he still felt the need to establish her as a dramatic character through an earlier appearance.)

Fifth, "Dr. Antonio" is Fellini's first color film. The mere fact of this is far less important than what he works out in terms of a color "aesthetic." He presents color as a world of richness, multiplicity, vitality, and freedom—the world, in effect, of Eros. Then he establishes black and white as a diminishment, an abstraction, a form of exclusion or "censorship"—hence associated with Dr. Antonio. In addition, he presents white as the embodiment of unity (the combination of all hues) in a world of color, while suggesting that in a world of black and white, white can only be part of a duality (the opposite or "negative" of black).

Given these basic distinctions, he works the entire film out in terms of a conflict between black and white and color. Every major negative development is set up as an intrusion of black and white into a color world. Dr. Antonio is introduced through black and white photos. Reality gives way to fiction through the mediation of a black and white movie. The billboard of Anita is a giant black and white "abstraction" which blocks the view of a color world. Antonio's vision, which occurs at night and consists of Anita's billboard-come-to-life is largely black and white.

To the extent that color remains, it loses its positive capabilities. The red of Antonio's bathrobe is singular, alienated, in the black and white world of his vision. No longer part of a multiple world of colors, it gets caught up in duality and becomes the color of aggression, violence, and domination. (Color here is forced to act like black and white.)

Fellini's discovery of color in "Dr. Antonio," and—perhaps more important—his discovery of the limitations of black and white, virtually ensured a permanent move to color as his vision became increasingly dynamic, rich, and affirmative. Though he momentarily reverted to black and white for $8\frac{1}{2}$ (he was intimidated by the problems of controlling the color process in "Dr. Antonio"), he returned to color for *Juliet* and has not abandoned it since.[9]

Sixth, "Dr. Antonio" is the first Fellini film to be thoroughly self-conscious about its medium. Fellini's manipulation of fictional form and his examination of "projection" as a filmic as well as a psychological problem reveal that he is no longer using his medium merely to tell stories—he is making it *part* of the story. In so doing, he is adding yet another dimension to his art, unifying it in yet another way. He is also en route to films like $8\frac{1}{2}$, *Director's Notebook*, *The Clowns*, and *Roma*, which, in taking the art of filmmaking as a principal subject, become profound investigations into the aesthetics of cinema.

Last of all, "The Temptations of Dr. Antonio" possesses a density and sophistication that clearly puts it in the company of the later films. The discontinuity in style and structure, the subtle diminishment of Eros, and the intricate process of fictionalization make "Dr. Antonio" a much more complex film, in terms of narrative technique, than even *La Dolce Vita*. (The complexity of the latter derived more from its length and thematic comprehensiveness than from narrative method.)

Moreover, it is the first film in which—by abandoning the three unities and thus eliminating dramatic continuity and exposition—Fellini begins to compress enormous narrative significance within each individual image. Within approximately five minutes of the film's beginning—through the black and white silent comedy—Fellini works out a series of narrative changes from potential wholeness to mere coupling to divorce that would have comprised major phases in earlier films. Although the presence of Antonio, who brings with him the conventional trappings of character, story, plot, and dramatic conflict, quickly dissipates such narrative compression, the opening of "Dr. Antonio" is clearly a sign of things to come. Films such as *Juliet of the Spirits* and *Satyricon* will work from beginning to end through the explosive succession of densely significant image-processes undiluted by the conventions of story line and exposition.

In conclusion, it might be said that with "The Temptations of Dr. Antonio" Fellini comes of age as a movie artist. He discovers the enormous expressive power of the individual moving image. He begins to explore the liberating potential of color. He recognizes that his medium *is* his story (to paraphrase McLuhan). And he attains a level of cinematic signification matched by few other directors. He is thus prepared to make a series of films, beginning with 8½, that not only expand the frontiers of cinematic expression but that see movie art as a crucial tool in the pursuit of spiritual and imaginative fulfillment.

To be continued . . .

Notes and References

Preface

1. William Carlos Williams, *Paterson* (New York: New Directions, 1963), author's note; my italics.
2. John Dewey, *Art as Experience* (New York: G. P. Putnam's, 1958), pp. 194–95.

Chapter One

1. See Cesare Zavattini, "Some Ideas on the Cinema," *Sight and Sound* (October 1953); reprinted in *Film: A Montage of Theories*, ed. Richard Dyer MacCann (New York, 1966).
2. See especially Peter Bondanella, "Early Fellini: *Variety Lights, The White Sheik*, and *I Vitelloni*," in *Federico Fellini: Essays in Criticism*, ed. Bondanella (New York, 1978), pp. 220–23; and Ben Lawton, "Italian Neorealism: A Mirror Construction of Reality," *Film Criticism* 3, no. 2 (1979):8–23. This entire issue of *Film Criticism* is devoted to neorealism and contains much useful material. The standard "introduction" to neorealism is, of course, Roy Armes, *Patterns of Realism: A Study of Italian Neorealist Cinema* (London: Tantivy Press, 1971). Peter Bondanella's *Italian Cinema: From Neorealism to the Present* (New York, 1983) provides a useful update on scholarly views of neorealism. (See especially chapters two to five.)
3. Williams, *Paterson*, p. 3.
4. For more extensive discussion of the problems of distance, alienation, and objectivity in both "A Matrimonial Agency" and Zavattini's theory, see Frank Burke, "Zavattini's Neorealism, Fellini's '*Un'agenzia matrimoniale*,' and the Limitations of Objectivity," *Proceedings of the Purdue University Fifth Annual Conference on Film* (West Lafayette, Ind., 1981), pp. 165–70.
5. *Fellini on Fellini*, ed. Anna Keel and Christian Strich, trans. Isabel Quigley (New York, 1976), pp. 52–53; hereafter cited in the text as *FF*.
6. Ernest Hemingway, *The Sun Also Rises* (New York: Scribner's, 1954), p. 148.

7.   Pierre Kast, "Giulietta and Federico: Visits With Fellini," *Cahiers du Cinéma in English*, no. 5 (1966); reprinted in *Interviews With Film Directors*, ed. Andrew Sarris (New York, 1967), p. 183; hereafter cited in the text as *K*.

8.   Zavattini, "Some Ideas," p. 228.

9.   Federico Fellini, "The Road Beyond Neorealism," in *Film*, ed. Mac-Cann, p. 379.

10.   "The Game of Truth," in Gilbert Salachas, *Federico Fellini: An Investigation Into His Films and Philosophy*, trans. Rosalie Siegel (New York, 1969), p. 114.

Chapter Two

1.   Charles Thomas Samuels, *Encountering Directors* (New York, 1972), p. 118.

2.   *Federico Fellini: Early Screenplays: Variety Lights, The White Sheik*, trans. Judith Green (New York, 1971), p. 60; hereafter cited in the text as *ES*.

3.   At first it might appear that he is back in touch with things, since he has rejoined Melina and his old troupe. However, while he seems to be reunited physically, he is clearly divorced mentally. And actually, a close look reveals him to be divorced even physically. He is alone on the station platform the first time we see him. He is the last one of the troupe to get on the train. The only member of the troupe with whom he associates is Melina. And, by the final shots, even she has disappeared, leaving him alone in the frame.

Chapter Three

1.   My negative view of the ending of *The White Sheik* concurs with Peter Bondanella's view. See "Early Fellini: *Variety Lights, The White Sheik*, and *I Vitelloni*," in *Essays in Criticism*, ed. Bondanella, pp. 232–33.

2.   Samuels, *Encountering Directors*, p. 125.

3.   "*Amarcord*: The Fascism Within Us: An Interview With Valerio Riva," in *Essays in Criticism*, ed. Bondanella, p. 21.

4.   For a somewhat different perspective on word and image, stasis and motion, in *The White Sheik*, see Stephen Snyder, "*The White Sheik*: Discovering the Story in the Medium," in *The 1977 Film Studies Annual: Part One, Explorations in National Cinemas* (Pleasantville, N.Y., 1977), pp. 100–110.

Chapter Four

1.   *Federico Fellini: Three Screenplays: I Vitelloni, Il Bidone, The Temptations of Dr. Antonio*, trans. Judith Green (New York, 1970), p. 14; hereafter cited in the text as *TS*.

2.   Fausto, distraught at being unable to find Sandra, tells Moraldo "If she doesn't come back, I'll kill myself." Moraldo replies with bitter sarcasm: "You

won't kill yourself, you're a coward" (ibid., 123). Moraldo's moralism has become so extreme that he criticizes Fausto for not being able to take his own life—rather than for his recent indiscretions.

3. Guido, of course, presages the main charcter of *8½* who, in one of his guises, is also a uniformed youth. The latter film will, however, liberate or "redeem" the trapped Guido of *I Vitelloni*. In each film, the principal problem is one of "guidance" (hence the name Guido). In *Vitelloni*, guidance becomes absolute control, and freedom is impossible. In *8½* Guido will develop the capacity for self-guidance and self-determination. Moreover, he will learn to outgrow his own penchant, as film director, to guide or control everyone else.

Chapter Five

1. Although the Italian title is "Un'agenzia matrimoniale," Fellini's episode is entitled "Love Cheerfully Arranged" in North American prints of *Love in the City*.

2. Quoted in Angelo Solmi, *Fellini*, trans. Elizabeth Greenwood (Atlantic Highlands, N.J., 1968), pp. 104–05.

3. Quotations from the film are taken from English subtitles and the English-language voice-over narration.

Chapter Six

1. Quoted in Solmi, *Fellini*, p. 116.

2. "The Long Interview: Tullio Kezich and Federico Fellini," in *Federico Fellini's Juliet of the Spirits*, ed. Tullio Kezich, trans. Howard Greenfield (New York, 1966), p. 30.

3. For further discussion of the road as both a positive and a negative symbol see Frank Burke, "Peckinpah's *Convoy* and the Tradition of the Open Road," *Film Studies: Proceedings of the Purdue University Sixth Annual Conference on Film* (West Lafayette, Ind., 1982), pp. 79–84.

4. My italics. Quotations from the dialogue are based on the Italian-language (subtitled) version of the film. In some cases, in the interests of precision, I have translated the dialogue myself rather than rely on the subtitles.

5. The name of the circus—Giraffa—also points to a gap between head and body at this point in the film.

6. "The Game of Truth," in Salachas, *Federico Fellini*, p. 114.

7. I recognize that my view of the final scene runs counter to the more common critical view that Zampanò is somehow awakened and redeemed at the end—a view which Fellini himself has tended to encourage by talking of the film in terms of enlightenment. All the evidence, it seems to me, is to the contrary. The film is, indeed, about an enlightenment (Gelsomina's), but about an enlightenment that is ultimately negated.

Chapter Seven

1.   Here the film differs sharply from the screenplay, which provided a reconciliation and thus allowed at least the illusion of a family life for Picasso to survive a bit longer.

2.   In the screenplay, as Augusto lies wounded, he says: "I'm never going to support anybody. . . . That's why I'm dying" (*TS*, 250), which links his failed attempt to swindle his partners with his desire to help Patrizia. With that clear indication of motive gone from the film, his final mention of Patrizia—"Oh, Patrizia, my baby girl" (ibid.)—comes across as a product of his delirium rather than as a clarification of why he has done what he has done.

Chapter Eight

1.   "On Producers," in Salachas, *Federico Fellini*, p. 105.

2.   Subtitle from the print of *Cabiria* distributed by the Canadian Film Institute.

3.   With regard to the religious or spiritual dimension of Fellini's vision—especially in *The Nights of Cabiria*—I strongly recommend André Bazin's marvelous essay, "*Cabiria:* The Voyage to the End of Neo-realism," in *What Is Cinema*, *II* (Berkeley, 1971), pp. 83–92, where he discusses Fellini's recurrent efforts to "angelize" his characters. Bazin's essay is reprinted in *Essays in Criticism*, ed. Bondanella, pp. 94–102. For further insight into the religious dimension of Fellini's vision in general, I recommend Charles B. Ketcham, *Federico Fellini: The Search for a New Mythology* (New York, 1976), passim, but especially p. 81.

4.   Unfortunately, this crucial question is not translated in subtitled prints of the film. My quotations of dialogue from the film are usually based on the Italian-language, subtitled version of *The Nights of Cabiria*. However, where the subtitles prove inadequate, I provide my own translation of the Italian.

5.   The fact that the choice is Cabiria's is clear from the way she responds to the Conjuror. Prior to the Maria-Oscar trance, when the Conjuror puts Cabiria under, she goes immediately limp, and her limpness is contrasted sharply with her aggression toward the crowd when "awake." But when the Conjuror says "Let me present Oscar," Cabiria—though momentarily immobilized by the Conjuror's influence—responds aggressively. She turns to the Conjuror in full control of her senses and asks quite forcefully: "I wonder . . . who is this Oscar?" When the Conjuror actually does "present" Oscar, Cabiria willingly closes her eyes and submits to the hypnotic trance.

6.   Salachas, *Federico Fellini*, p. 102.

7.   For some helpful comments on the function of music in *The Nights of Cabiria* see Claudia Gorbman, "Music as Salvation: Notes on Fellini and Rota," *Film Quarterly* 28, no. 3 (1974–75):17–25; reprinted in *Essays in Criticism*, ed. Bondanella, pp. 80–94.

Chapter Nine

1.   The script for this project has just been published in English. See *Federico Fellini: Moraldo in the City and A Journey with Anita*, ed. and trans. John C. Stubbs (Urbana, Ill., 1983).

2.   *La Dolce Vita*, trans. Oscar DeLiso and Bernard Shir-Cliff (New York, 1961), p. 14; hereafter cited in the text as *DV*. In instances where the subtitles for the Italian-language print are accurate and the screenplay edition is not, I will quote from the subtitles and indicate that I am doing so with an *S* in the text. In instances in which neither the screenplay nor the subtitled version is correct, I will provide my own translation, indicating so with a *T* in the text.

3.   Marianne is unnamed in the movie, but for ease of reference I will use the name given her in the screenplay.

4.   Marcello notes that she is from the same part of the country and that she came to Rome "to make a fortune too" (*DV*, 257).

5.   *Fellini on Fellini*, p. 157.

Chapter Ten

1.   My concern both in this chapter and elsewhere in the book has been with the way Fellini's imaginative development has manifested itself solely in his movies. However, I would direct the reader to the two scripted projects by Fellini—"Moraldo in the City" and "A Journey With Anita"—which have just been edited and translated by John C. Stubbs. They reveal that, as early as 1954, Fellini was beginning to tell stories of affirmation, liberation.

2.   Erich Neumann, *The Origins and History of Consciousness*, trans. R. F. C. Hull, Bollingen Series, no. 42 (Princeton, N.J.: Princeton University Press, 1970), p. 363.

Chapter Eleven

1.   Eros's voice-over is dubbed in English even in subtitled (Italian-language) prints, so this quotation is directly from dubbing. Other quotations from the dialogue are also from dubbing, which has been checked for accuracy against the Italian-language prints.

2.   See H. J. Rose, *A Handbook of Greek Mythology Including Its Extension to Rome* (New York: E. P. Dutton, 1959), p. 123, and Michael Grant, *Myths of the Greeks and Romans* (New York: New American Library, 1962), pp. 96–97.

3.   Both St. Anthony and the monastic tradition are, of course, held in high regard in orthodox Catholic tradition. They are seen as models of spiritual will overcoming worldliness. However, the film tends to place them in a different light—as models of "spiritual" development bought at the expense of love or relat-

edness. They become symptomatic of a civilization created through repression. (So, for that matter, does the symbology of St. George).

4.   The only contact between the girl and others occurs during her first appearance, when Eros still presides as a link between the divine and the human. Even here, the contact is purely mechanical (a waiter serves her ice cream), and she sits by herself, unnoticed by Antonio and his luncheon companions. In her second appearance, she and Antonio are alone in front of the billboard, but Antonio, in his absorption with Anita, does not see her until she nearly runs him over— then he does everything he can to avoid her. In her third appearance, she is isolated on screen and never related to anyone else, even though she appears in the midst of a carnival with crowds of people around. Here Antonio's absorption is so complete (this is the ink-throwing scene) that there is no chance of his becoming aware of the girl.

5.   One might say that the film as a whole, precisely because it is a film, necessarily begins in fiction and is, therefore, a denial of reality. However, Fellini, particularly in his later work, sees movie art as having the potential to break down divisions between reality and illusion, viewer and viewed. (See my discussion of the end of *The Nights of Cabiria*, chapter 8.) Moreover, he would argue that, under the best circumstances, film offers the viewer not fiction but reality infused with imagination—and that a creative spectator is not a mere consumer of fictions, he or she is a co-creator, co-envisioner of this new and heightened reality. (For some interesting remarks by Fellini on the film experience and on the active role of the viewer, see Gideon Bachman, "Federico Fellini: 'The Cinema Seen as A Woman . . . ,'" *Film Quarterly* 34, no. 2 [1980–81], especially p. 5.) The kind of division that occurs in "Dr. Antonio" between reality and fiction occurs only because all possibility for unity has been lost.

6.   Quoted by Grant, *Myths*, p. 97.

7.   I use the word "seemingly" because Fellini is *always* telling a story, no matter how experimental and discontinuous his narrative method becomes.

8.   The scene of Antonio's associates has not been included in the dubbed prints that I have seen; it apparently exists only in subtitled versions. This is most unfortunate. Its hypnagogic style anticipates much of later Fellini and, in particular, the dream style of *Juliet of the Spirits*.

9.   Apparently, in *La Nave Va* (his film in production at the time of this writing) Fellini is using color film, then draining the color out of it, in order to accentuate the limitations of a world without color. (The story is set at the outbreak of World War I and is, from all accounts, quite negative.)

Selected Bibliography

1. Screenplays

La Dolce Vita. Translated by Oscar DeLiso and Bernard Shir-Cliff. New York: Ballantine Books, 1961.

Federico Fellini: Early Screenplays: Variety Lights, The White Sheik. Translated by Judith Green. New York: Grossman, 1971.

Federico Fellini: Three Screenplays: I Vitelloni, Il Bidone, The Temptations of Dr. Antonio. Translated by Judith Green. New York: Grossman, 1970.

Moraldo in the City and A Journey With Anita. Edited and translated by John C. Stubbs. Urbana: University of Illinois Press, 1983. Unrealized projects.

La Strada. Translated by Cicely Gittes. A manuscript copy is on file at the American Film Institute Library, 501 Doheny Road, Beverly Hills, Calif. 90210.

2. Interviews/Writings by Fellini

"Federico Fellini: An Interview." *Film: Book I*. Edited by Robert Hughes. New York: Grove Press, 1959, pp. 97–105. Reprinted as "The Road Beyond Neorealism," in *Film: A Montage of Theories*. Edited by Richard Dyer MacCann. New York: E. P. Dutton, 1966, pp. 377–84. Fellini discusses what motivates him to make a movie, how he works, and what neorealism and his work with Rossellini meant to him.

KAST, PIERRE. "Giulietta and Federico: Visits With Fellini." *Cahiers du Cinéma in English*, no. 5 (1966), pp. 24–33. Reprinted in *Interviews With Film Directors*. Edited by Andrew Sarris. New York: Bobbs-Merrill, 1967, pp. 176–92. Extensive discussion covering Fellini's themes, his use of color, his concern with "individuation," and the symbolic role of the female in that process.

KEEL, ANNA, and STRICH, CHRISTIAN, eds. *Fellini on Fellini*. Translated by Isabel Quigley. New York: Dell, 1976. An excellent, 166-page collection of interview materials and writings by Fellini. Particularly notable are the lengthy biographical piece, "Rimini, My Home Town," and Fellini's descriptions of how he goes about preparing and casting his movies.

KEZICH, TULLIO. "The Long Interview: Tullio Kezich and Federico Fellini." In *Federico Fellini's Juliet of the Spirits*. Edited by Tullio Kezich. Translated by Howard Greenfield. New York: Ballantine Books, 1966, pp. 17–64. Covers much of the same material as the Kast interview but in greater detail. Probes more deeply into Fellini's vision as a whole and into the aesthetic dimension of his work.

"Playboy Interview: Federico Fellini.*" Playboy* 13, no. 2 (February 1966):55–66. Wide-ranging discussion of the theme of liberation as it applies to *8½* and *Juliet of the Spirits.*

Ross, Lilian. "Profiles: 10½.*" New Yorker* 41, no. 37 (30 October 1965):63–107. A profile of Fellini done in the form of a screenplay. Casual, informative discussion, reminiscences, comments on Fellini's then most recent film, *Juliet of the Spirits.*

Samuels, Charles Thomas. *Encountering Directors.* New York: G. P. Putnam's, 1972, pp. 117–41. Fellini interviewed about his entire career. While fending off Samuels's opionated intellectualizations, Fellini is goaded into some unusually direct statements about his intentions and his work.

SECONDARY SOURCES

1. Bibliographies

Price, Barbara Anne, and Price, Theodore. *Federico Fellini: An Annotated International Bibliography.* Metuchen, N.J.: Scarecrow Press, 1978. A 282-page listing of material published by and about Fellini in ten languages. Filmography and credits.

Stubbs, John C., with Constance D. Markey and Marc Lenzini. *Federico Fellini: A Guide to References and Resources.* Boston: G. K. Hall, 1978. A 346-page compilation which includes bibliographical information on material published by and about Fellini in English, French, and Italian as well as a biographical section and a critical overview of Fellini's films. Includes filmography, credits, and extensive synopses of the films.

2. Books

Agel, Geneviève. *Les chemins de Fellini.* Paris: Éditions du Cerf, 1956. A study of the themes and Christian symbolism of Fellini's early films through *Il Bidone.* Extremely sensitive to Fellini's vision and the spirit of his films. Fellini has singled this out as a worthwhile discussion of his movies. Agel's chapter on *Il Bidone* is reprinted in Bondanella's *Essays in Criticism* (see below).

Betti, Liliana. *Fellini.* Translated by Joachim Neugroschel. Boston: Little, Brown, 1979. An amusing and informative personal portrait of Fellini by a woman who has worked with him for twenty years.

Bondanella, Peter, ed. *Federico Fellini: Essays in Criticism.* Oxford: Oxford University Press, 1978. A selection of the best essays and interview materials (often translated from French and Italian) available on Fellini. The best point of departure (other than the films themselves) for studying Fellini.

Budgen, Suzanne. *Fellini.* London: British Film Institute, 1966. An illuminating thematic study of Fellini's work through *Juliet of the Spirits.* Includes interview material and a translation of a scene from the script of *La Strada.* Remains the best study of Fellini in English by a single author.

Costello, Donald P. *Fellini's Road.* Notre Dame: University of Notre Dame Press, 1983. An extensive discussion of *La Strada, La Dolce Vita, 8½,* and *Juliet of the Spirits,* using the motif of the road as a departure point in examining the Fellinian "search for self." Appeared after the text of my study was completed.

KETCHAM, CHARLES B. *Federico Fellini: The Search for a New Mythology.* New York: Paulist Press, 1976. An examination of Fellini's religious sensibility, within a Catholic context, with special attention to *La Strada, La Dolce Vita,* and *8½.*

MURRAY, EDWARD. *Fellini the Artist.* New York: Frederick Ungar, 1976. A discussion of Fellini's feature films from *The White Sheik* through *Amarcord.* Mostly a recounting of the plots, occasionally faulty in detail. Includes a number of interesting quotations from Fellini which, unfortunately, are not documented.

RONDI, BRUNELLO. *Il Cinema di Fellini.* Rome: Edizioni di Bianco e Nero. 1965. Lengthy discussions of all Fellini's films from *Variety Lights* through *Juliet of the Spirits* by a close collaborator and friend. Marvelous insight into Fellini the man and Fellini the artist.

ROSENTHAL, STUART. *The Cinema of Federico Fellini.* South Brunswick, N.J.: A. S. Barnes, 1976. Amply illustrated thematic and stylistic study of Fellini's films through *Amarcord.* Emphasis on Fellini's vision and on the role of spectacle, symbolism, and characterization in his work.

SALACHAS, GILBERT. *Federico Fellini: An Investigation Into His Films and Philosophy.* Translated by Rosalie Siegel. New York: Crown Publishers, 1969. Covers Fellini's work through *Juliet of the Spirits.* Helpful biographical information and interview material. Includes excerpts from screenplays and treatments as well as critical responses to the early films.

SOLMI, ANGELO. *Fellini.* Translated by Elizabeth Greenwood. Atlantic Highlands, N.J.: Humanities Press, 1968. A sympathetic thematic introduction to Fellini's films through *8½.* Particularly useful for information on Fellini's life before he became a filmmaker—and for production information on the films.

STRICH, CHRISTIAN, ed. *Fellini's Films.* New York: Putnam's, 1977. Four hundred photographs, many in color, from Fellini's films from *Variety Lights* through *Casanova.* A foreword by George Simenon, synopses of the films, cast, and credits. A beautiful edition.

3. Chapters from books

BAZIN, ANDRÉ. "*Cabiria:* The Voyage to the End of Neorealism." In *What Is Cinema, II.* Translated by Hugh Gray. Berkeley: University of California Press, 1971, pp. 83–92. Reprinted in Bondanella's *Essays in Criticism* (see above). An extraordinarily sensitive discussion of the spiritual nature of Fellini's "neorealism"—his ability to derive hidden meaning from the real. Also talks of Fellini's innovations in liberating plot from pure causality.

BONDANELLA, PETER. "The Break with Neorealism: Rossellini in Transition, Early Antonioni and Fellini," "The Mature *Auteurs*: New Dimensions in Film Narrative with Visconti, Antonioni, and Fellini," "Politics and Ideology in the Contemporary Italian Cinema." In *Italian Cinema: From Neorealism to the Present.* New York: Frederick Ungar, 1983. See especially pp. 113–41, 228–52, 320–22. The first two chapters noted above discuss the films covered in this book—providing solid links between Fellini and neorealism and tracing his development beyond it.

HARCOURT, PETER. "The Secret Life of Federico Fellini." In *Six European Directors: Essays on the Meaning of Film Style*. Baltimore: Penguin, 1974, pp. 183–213. This is an updated version of an essay of the same title in *Film Quarterly* 19, no. 3 (1966):4–13, 19. Reprinted in Bondanella's *Essays in Criticism* (see above). Discusses Fellini's work through *Satyricon*. Sees him as a "subliminal," instinctual, artist who works more in the manner of a painter than a conventional narrative artist. Emphasizes the "restlessness of movement" and the journey in Fellini's work.

ORTMAYER, ROGER. "Fellini's Film Journey." In *Three European Directors: Truffaut, Fellini, Bunuel*. Edited by James M. Wall. Grand Rapids, Mich.: Wm. B. Eerdmans Publishing Co., 1973, pp. 65–108. Focuses on *La Strada, Juliet of the Spirits*, and *Satyricon*. An attempt to relate Fellini's vision to changes in contemporary worldview. Addresses aesthetic values of motion, communication, and color in Fellini. Very insightful.

RICHARDSON, ROBERT. "Wastelands: The Breakdown of Order." In *Literature and Film*. Bloomington: Indiana Univ. Press, 1969, pp. 106–16. Reprinted in Bondanella's *Essays in Criticism* (see above). Relates *La Dolce Vita* to T. S. Eliot's *The Wasteland* in terms of fragmentation, discontinuity in narrative style, modernism, and the breakdown of tradition.

TAYLOR, JOHN RUSSELL. *Cinema Eye, Cinema Ear*. New York: Hill & Wang, 1964, pp. 15–51. A sympathetic overview of Fellini's work from *Variety Lights* through *8½*. Discusses Fellini's concern with "inner reality," the "magical tenderness" of his vision, the role of the sea, the square, and the night versus day in his films. Prizes Fellini above all else for the "feeling of instantaneous creation" that emerges from his work.

4. Articles

BAZIN, ANDRÉ. "*La Strada*." *Cross Currents* 6, no. 3 (1956): 200–203. Reprinted in Bondanella's *Essays in Criticism* (see above). Calls *La Strada* a "phenomenology of the soul." Expands the concept of neorealism to incorporate Fellini's vision of the mythic yet real.

BONDANELLA, PETER. "Early Fellini: *Variety Lights, The White Sheik*, and *I Vitelloni*." In Bondanella's *Essays in Criticism* (see above). Excellent thematic analysis of Fellini's first three films, relating them (largely by way of contrast) to neorealism.

BURKE, FRANK. "Fellini's Drive for Individuation." *Southwest Review* 64, no. 1 (1979):68–84. Surveys Fellini's career from *Variety Lights* through *Roma*, seeking to demonstrate the growing creativity of Fellini's characters and filmworld. Sees Fellini's imagination undergoing a process of individuation, along with his characters.

———. "Zavattini's Neorealism, Fellini's '*Un'agenzia matrimoniale*,' and the Limitations of Objectivity." In *Proceedings of the Purdue University Fifth Annual Conference on Film*. West Lafayette, Ind.: Purdue Office of Publications, 1981, pp. 165–70. An examination of Fellini's use of the reporter as main character in this short film to undercut Zavattini's emphasis on "objective reportage."

EASON, PATRICK. "Notes on Double Structure and the Films of Fellini." *Cinema* (London) 2 (1969):22–24. A structuralist, "binary" approach to Fellini, focusing on *La Strada, Il Bidone*, and *8½*.

GORBMAN, CLAUDIA. "Music as Salvation: Notes on Fellini and Rota." *Film Quarterly* 28, no. 2 (1974–75):17–25. Extremely interesting discussion of the relationship of music (and of silence) to the themes and structure of *The Nights of Cabiria* (with some reference to *La Strada*). Reprinted in Bondanella's *Essays in Criticism* (see above).

HOLLAND, NORMAN. "The Follies Fellini." *Hudson Review* 14, no. 3 (1961):425–31. Reprinted in *Renaissance of the Film*. Edited by Julius Bellone. New York: Collier-Macmillan, 1970. Illuminating discussion of men versus women, seeing versus hearing, and the mythic dimension in *La Dolce Vita*.

SNYDER, STEPHEN. "*The White Sheik*: Discovering the Story in the Medium." In *The 1977 Film Studies Annual: Part One, Explorations in National Cinemas*, Pleasantville, N.Y.: Redgrave Publishing, 1977, pp. 100–110. Sees *The White Sheik* in self-reflexive terms—as a film that plays image and word, stasis and motion, off against each other to generate meaning in specifically cinematic ways.

SWADOS, HARVEY. "*La Strada:* Realism and the Comedy of Poverty." *Yale French Studies* 17 (Summer 1956):38–43. Relates *La Strada* to neorealism and Masina to Charlie Chaplin in asserting the universal validity of Fellini's presentation of victims of poverty.

5. Documentaries about Fellini

Ciao Federico! Directed by Gideon Bachman. Color, 60 minutes, 1970. Distributed by Macmillan/Audio Brandon Films, Mt. Vernon, New York. An informative, though opinionated view of Fellini, shot during the making of *Satyricon*. Its presentation of Fellini's working methods and relationships while on the set is quite interesting.

Fellini: The Director as Creator. Edited by Michael Misch. Black and white, 27 minutes, 1970. Distributed by Harold Mantell, Inc., New York City. Fellini at work on *Juliet of the Spirits*. Thorough presentation of Fellini's way of getting a film made. More objective than *Ciao Federico!*

Wizards, Clowns, and Honest Liars. Produced and distributed by Roger Ailes Associates, New York City. Narrated by John Huddy. Color, 48 minutes, 1978. Illustrated abundantly with clips from Fellini's films, this documentary offers a sensitive overview of Fellini's career, as well as interview material and on-the-set footage obtained during the making of *Casanova*.

Filmography (1950–62)

Editor's note: Rental and sale of films for noncommercial exhibition and videotapes of films for home showing is in such an uncertain state as this book goes to press that we provide no information about possible sources of copies of Fellini's films. Those seeking information should get in touch with Films, Inc., Wilmette, Illinois, which at the time this book was completed, principally controlled distribution of Fellini's early films.

VARIETY LIGHTS (Capitolium Film, 1950)
Producers: Alberto Lattuada and Federico Fellini
Co-director: Lattuada
Screenplay: Lattuada, Fellini, Ennio Flaiano, Tullio Pinelli; based on a story by Fellini
Cinematographer: Otello Martelli
Sets: Aldo Buzzi
Music: Felice Lattuada
Editor: Mario Bonotti
Cast: Peppino De Filippo (Checco Dalmonte), Carla del Poggio (Liliana), Giulietta Masina (Melina Amour), John Kitzmiller (Johnny, the trumpet player), Folco Lulli (Conti), Franca Valeri (the designer), Carlo Romano (Renzo, the lawyer), Silvio Bagolini (the journalist), Dante Maggio (Remo, the comedian), Giulio Cali (Edison Will), Gina Mascetti (Valeria Del Sole)
Running Time: 93 minutes
Released: Italy, 1950; United States, 6 May 1965, New Yorker Theater, New York

THE WHITE SHEIK (PDC-OFI, 1952)
Producer: Luigi Rovere
Assistant Director: Stefano Ubezio
Screenplay: Fellini, Ennio Flaiano, Tullio Pinelli; based on a story by Michelangelo Antonioni, Fellini, and Pinelli
Cinematographer: Arturo Gallea
Sets: Raffaelo Tolfo
Music: Nino Rota
Sound: Armando Grilli, Walfredo Traversari
Editor: Rolando Benedetti
Production Manager: Enzo Provenzale

138

Cast: Alberto Sordi (Fernando Rivoli, the White Sheik), Brunella Bovo (Wanda
Giardino Cavalli), Leopoldo Trieste (Ivan Cavalli), Giulietta Masina (Cabiria),
Lilia Landi (Felga), Ernesto Almirante (Director), Fanny Marchio (Marilena
Vellardi), Gina Mascetti (the Sheik's wife)
Running Time: 86 minutes
Released: Italy, first showing at Venice Film Festival, Spring 1952; United States,
25 April 1956, 55th St. Playhouse, New York

I VITELLONI (Peg Films, Cité Films, 1953)
Producer: Lorenzo Pegoraro
Screenplay: Fellini, Ennio Flaiano, Tullio Pinelli
Cinematographer: Otello Martelli, Luciano Trasatti, Carlo Carlini
Sets: Mario Chiari
Music: Nino Rota
Editor: Rolando Benedetti
Production Director: Luigi Giacosi
Cast: Franco Interlenghi (Moraldo), Franco Fabrizi (Fausto), Alberto Sordi (Al-
berto), Leopoldo Trieste (Leopoldo), Riccardo Fellini (Riccardo), Eleonora
Ruffo (Sandra), Lida Baarova (Giulia, Michele's wife), Carlo Romano (Mich-
ele), Arlette Sauvage (woman in the cinema), Maja Nipora (actress), Jean Bro-
chard (Fausto's father), Claude Farell (Alberto's sister), Enrico Viarisio (San-
dra's father), Paola Borboni (Sandra's mother)
Running Time: 104 minutes
Released: Italy, first shown at 1953 Venice Film Festival; United States, 23 October 1956, 55th St. Playhouse, New York

"A MATRIMONIAL AGENCY" (Episode in *Love in the City*; other episodes by Risi,
Antonioni, Lattuada, Moselli and Zavattini, Lizzani; Faro Films, 1953)
Producers: Cesare Zavattini, Renato Ghione, Marco Ferreri
Screenplay: Fellini, Tullio Pinelli
Cinematographer: Gianni di Venanzo
Sets: Gianni Polidori
Music: Mario Nascimbene
Editor: Eraldo Da Roma
Cast: Antonio Cifariello (reporter), Livia Venturini (Rosanna), and nonprofessional
actors from the Centro sperimentale di cinematografia in Rome
Running Time: 18 minutes
Released: Italy, 1953; United States, 19 April 1961

LA STRADA (Carlo Ponti, Dino De Laurentiis, 1954)
Assistant Director: Moraldo Rossi
Screenplay: Fellini, Tullio Pinelli, Ennio Flaiano
Cinematographer: Otello Martelli
Sets: Mario Ravesco
Costumes: M. Marinari
Artistic Collaborators: Brunello Rondi, Paolo Nuzzi
Music: Nino Rota

Editor: Leo Cattozzo
Assistant Editor: Lina Caterini
Sound: A. Calpini
Director of Production: Luigi Giacosi
Special effects: E. Trani
Cast: Giulietta Masina (Gelsomina), Anthony Quinn (Zampanò), Richard Basehart
    (Il matto), Aldo Silvani (Colombaioni), Marcella Rovera (the widow), Livia
    Venturini (the nun)
Running Time: 107 minutes
Released: Italy, first shown 11 September 1954 at the Venice Film Festival; United
    States, 16 July 1956, Trans-Lux, 52nd Street, New York

IL BIDONE (Titanus-S.G.C., also released in the United States as *The Swindle,*
    1955)
Assistant Directors: Moraldo Rossi, Narciso Vicario
Assistants to the Director: Dominique Delouche, Paolo Nuzzi
Screenplay: Fellini, Ennio Flaiano, Tullio Pinelli
Cinematographer: Otello Martelli
Cameramen: Roberto Gerardi, Arturo Zavattini
Artistic Collaborator: Brunello Rondi
Sets and Costumes: Dario Cecchi
Decorator: Massimiliano Capriccioli
Music: Nino Rota
Sound: Giovanni Rossi
Editors: Mario Serandrei, Giuseppe Vari
Production Director: Giuseppe Colizzi
Cast: Broderick Crawford (Augusto), Richard Basehart (Picasso), Franco Fabrizi
    (Roberto), Giulietta Masina (Iris), Giacomo Gabrielli (Vargas), Alberto de
    Amicis (Rinaldo), Lorella de Luca (Patrizia), Irene Cefaro (Marisa), Sue Ellen
    Blake (Anna), Xenia Valderi (Luciana), Maria Zanoli (Stella Fiorina)
Running Time: 92 minutes
Released: Italy, 10 September 1955 at Venice Film Festival; United States, 1963,
    in San Francisco

THE NIGHTS OF CABIRIA (Dino De Laurentiis, 1956; also released in the United
    States as *Cabiria*)
Assistant Directors: Moraldo Rossi, Dominique Delouche
Screenplay: Fellini, Ennio Flaiano, Tullio Pinelli
Additional Dialogue: Pier Paolo Pasolini
Cinematographer: Aldo Toni, Otello Martelli
Sets and Costumes: Piero Gherardi
Music: Nino Rota
Sound: Roy Mangano
Editor: Leo Cattozzo
Production Director: Luigi De Laurentiis
Cast: Giulietta Masina (Cabiria), Amedeo Nazzari (the actor), François Perier (Os-
    car), Franca Marzi (Wanda), Dorian Gray (Jessy), Aldo Silvani (the hypnotist),
    Franco Fabrizi (Giorgio), Mario Passante (crippled uncle)

Running Time: 110 minutes
Released: Italy, first shown at Cannes Film Festival in March 1956 but distribution
in Italy did not begin until October 1957; United States, 28 October 1957,
Fine Arts Theater, New York

LA DOLCE VITA (Riama Film, Pathé Consortium Cinéma, 1960)
Producers: Giuseppe Amato, Angelo Rizzoli
Assistant Directors: Guidarino Guidi, Paolo Nuzzi, Dominique Delouche
Screenplay: Fellini, Tullio Pinelli, Ennio Flaiano, Brunello Rondi; from a story by
Fellini, Pinelli, and Flaiano
Cinematographer: Otello Martelli
Art Director: Piero Gherardi
Artistic Collaborator: Brunello Rondi
Music: Nino Rota
Sound: Agostino Moretti
Editor: Leo Cattozzo
Production Directors: Manlio M. Moretti, Nello Meniconi
Executive Producer: Franco Magli
Cast: Marcello Mastroianni (Marcello Rubini), Walter Santesso (Paparazzo), An-
ouk Aimée (Maddalena), Adriana Moneta (prostitute), Yvonne Fourneaux
(Emma), Anita Ekberg (Sylvia), Harriet White (Edna, Sylvia's secretary),
Carlo Di Maggio (Totò Scalise, the producer), Lex Barker (Robert, Sylvia's
fiancé), Alan Dijon (Frankie Stout), Alain Cuny (Steiner), Reneé Longarini
(Mrs. Steiner), Valeria Ciangottini (Paola), Annibale Ninchi (Marcello's
father), Magali Noël (Fanny), Nico Otzak (Nico), Prince Vadim Wolkonsky
(Prince Mascalchi), Audrey MacDonald (Jane), Nadia Gray (Nadia), Jacques
Sernas (matinee idol), Laura Betti (Laura), Riccardo Garrone (Riccardo),
Franca Pasutt (Pasutt)
Running Time: 180 minutes
Released: Italy, February 1960; United States, 19 April 1961, Henry Miller's
Theater, New York

"THE TEMPTATIONS OF DR. ANTONIO" (Episode in *Boccaccio '70*; other episodes
by Visconti, DeSica, Monicelli; Cineriz, 1962)
Producer: Carlo Ponti, Antonio Cervi
Screenplay: Fellini, Ennio Flaiano, Tullio Pinelli, with the collaboration of Bru-
nello Rondi and Goffredo Parise
Cinematographer: Otello Martelli (Eastmancolor)
Art Direction: Piero Zuffi
Music: Nino Rota
Editor: Leo Cattozzo
Cast: Peppino De Filippo (Dr. Antonio Mazzuolo), Anita Ekberg (Anita), Antonio
Acqua (government official), Donatella Della Nora (Mazzuolo's sister), Elean-
ora Maggi (Cupid)
Running Time: 70 minutes (approximately)
Released: Italy, 22 February 1962; United States, 26 June 1962, Cinemas 1 and 2,
New York

Index

Amore in Città (Love in the City), 31
Anthony, St., 116, 131–32n3
Antonioni, Michelangelo, 3, 13, 31
Aristotle, 107

Bach, Johann Sebastian, 91
Barnes, Jake (*The Sun Also Rises*), 2
Beethoven, Ludwig van, 73
Boccaccio '70, 115

Cabiria (Italian silent film), 69
Cardinale, Claudia, 124
Cupid, 117–18

Dante Alighieri, 85
De Filippo, Peppino, 9
DeSica, Vittorio, 1, 3, 115
Documentary method, 1, 2, 4, 31
Dog's Heart, A, 3

Ekberg, Anita, 9, 115, 117, 119, 120, 121,
    122, 123, 124
Eliot, T.S., 85
Eros (as god, not Fellini character), 115,
    116, 122

Fabrizi, Aldo, 7
Fascism, 2, 4, 24
Fellini, Federico
    and film aesthetics, 16–18, 109, 124–25
    imaginative development of, 3, 26–28,
        34–35, 53, 65–66, 82–83, *101–13*,
        122–25
    motivating impulses of, 2–5
    narrative and filmmaking methods of, 2,
        53, *107–12*, 113, 123–25; camera
        usage, 7, 10, 82, 96–97, 99, 109, 111–
        12, 113, 115; casting, 5;

characterization, 27–28, 35, 38, 53,
    82–83, 108–109, 123–24; color, 124,
    132n9; plot, 53, 107–08, 113; voice-
    over narration, 28, 32, 34, 35, 102,
    104–05, 115–19, 122
    and neorealism, 1–5, 31, 34
    and self-reflexivity, 10, 16–18, 61, 72–
        73, 109, 118–20, 124–25, 132n5

THEMATIC CONCERNS AND
    MOTIFS:
    absence, and growth or
        spiritualization, 73, 82, 96–97, 104;
        as loss, 37, 38, 50, 52, 59, 62, 104
    abstraction (*see also* illusion): in "A
        Matrimonial Agency," 32, 33; in *La
        Strada*, 42, 46, 47, 48, 50, 105; in
        "The Temptations of Dr. Antonio,"
        119, 120, 124; in *The White Sheik*,
        14
    alienation, 2, 16, 27, 103, 122; in *Il
        Bidone*, 58, 59, 60, 102; in *La
        Dolce Vita*, 35, 87, 112; in "A
        Matrimonial Agency," 112; in *The
        Nights of Cabiria*, 72, 81; in *La
        Strada*, 37, 41; in "The
        Temptations of Dr. Antonio," 116,
        122, 124; in *I Vitelloni*, 103
    annulment (*see also* negation): 16,
        93–96, 98, 99
    art and artifice, 4; in *Il Bidone*, 55,
        61; in *La Dolce Vita*, 89, 91; in *The
        Nights of Cabiria*, 72–73, 75, 76,
        77, 78; in *La Strada*, 37, 38–45; in
        "The Temptations of Dr. Antonio,"
        116, 117, 118–20; in *Variety
        Lights*, 7–10; in *I Vitelloni*, 24; in
        The White Sheik, 13–14, 16–17

authoritarianism (male authority).
    See institutionalism
Catholicism: 74, 75; and illusion, 14,
    24, 43, 46, 47–48, 57, 70, 88–89;
    and institutionalism, 14, 18, 23,
    25, 41, 43, 46, 47, 48, 70, 75, 115,
    116; and materialism, 57, 58
circularity (vs. linearity); 105–06
circus, the. *See* art and artifice
civilization: and false consciousness,
    38–53; and repression, 38–40, 42–
    43
communication, lack of. *See* love,
    absence, illusion, or loss of;
    marriage, and the absence of love
consciousness: development or
    transformation of (*see also*
    spiritualization), 2, 3, 4, 5, 39, 40–
    44, 71–75, 77–82, 101–107, 112;
    false or alienated, 2, 31–32, 38–50,
    40–44, 45, 56, 63–64, 112, 122;
    lack, loss, or failure of, 9, 14, 21–
    22, 26, 38, 43–50, 52, 53, 59, 63,
    85–96, 101, 102, 112, 118, 122;
    repression of, 38, 40, 41, 44, 52,
    56, 62, 93–94, 102, 112
conventionality (conformity): 5, 95; in
    "A Matrimonial Agency," 31, 33,
    34; in *La Strada*, 37, 38, 39, 41–44,
    46–47, 48; in "The Temptations of
    Dr. Antonio," 123, 125; in *Variety
    Lights*, 7, 101, 108; in *I Vitelloni*,
    21–26, 27, 28, 95, 108; in *The
    White Sheik*, 14–16, 101, 108, 110
creative experience (*see also*:
    consciousness, development or
    transformation of; imagination;
    spiritualization): 3, 17, 37, 38, 65,
    70, 75, 76, 77, 91, *101–107*, 123
dependency: in *Il Bidone*, 56, 59, 60,
    63; in *La Dolce Vita*, 88, 92, 93;
    and marriage, 16, 23; in "A
    Matrimonial Agency," 31; in *The
    Nights of Cabiria*, 70; and the
    provinces, 15; in *La Strada*, 43–44,
    45, 47; in *Variety Lights*, 101; in *I
    Vitelloni*, 21, 22, 23–24, 26; in *The
    White Sheik*, 15–16, 17, 101
detachment (objectivity): 2, 25, 31; in
    Il Bidone, 56, 62; in *La Dolce Vita*,
    86, 88, 89–90, 91, 92; in "A
    Matrimonial Agency," 31, 32, 34,
    35; in *La Strada*, 47–48

division (polarity): 16, 17–18, 32–34,
    38, 39–50, 57, 74, 86, 116–18, 124
ego-differentiation, 101–02, 103
egoism, 9, 10, 14; transcendence of,
    81
enlightenment. *See* consciousness,
    development or transformation of;
    spiritualization
escapism. *See* illusion
exile (imagery of): 57, 58, 60, 61–62,
    64
family, absence, loss, or illusion of: 8,
    24–25, 27, 35, 39, 43, 47–48, 52,
    57–63, 103; and dependency, 15–
    16, 23–24, 26, 110; and
    institutionalism, 15–16, 23–24
fantasy. *See* illusion
film, medium of: 16–18, 72–73, 86,
    87, 94, 109, 113, 120, 124–25,
    132n5
fragmentation: 2, 27–28, 38, 55, 122
givenness (vs. possibility): 73, 87, 91,
    92, 96, 103–04, 117
identity, lack or loss of: in *Il Bidone*,
    56, 57, 58, 59; in *La Dolce Vita*, 94;
    in *The Nights of Cabiria*, 71; in *La
    Strada*, 38–50, 52, 59; in "The
    Temptations of Dr. Antonio," 120;
    in *Variety Lights*, 8–9; in *I
    Vitelloni*, 21, 26; in *The White
    Sheik*, 14, 17, 18, 104
illusion: and art or artifice, 7–10, 13–
    14, 16–17, 37, 38–45, 117, 118–20;
    in *Il Bidone*, 55, 56–57, 58, 61, 63,
    64, 65; bourgeois, 1–2, 3, 4, 5, 70;
    and Catholicism, 14, 24, 43, 46,
    47–48, 57, 70; in *La Dolce Vita*,
    112; and Fascism, 1–2, 24; and
    marriage, 13, 16, 48, 70, 104, 105;
    in "A Matrimonial Agency," 34,
    102; in *The Nights of Cabiria*, 70,
    73, 77, 104; and Rome, 8, 13, 14–
    15, 43; in *La Strada*, 37, 40–45, 46,
    47, 48; in "The Temptations of Dr.
    Antonio," 116, 117, 118–20, 122; in
    Variety Lights, 7–10, 101; in *I
    Vitelloni*, 21, 24, 26; in *The White
    Sheik*, 2, 13–14, 16–18, 101, 104
imagination: 3, 4, 27, 35, 38, 40, 44,
    72, 75, 76, 77, 90, 104, 108, 109,
    117, 123
individuation (*see also* consciousness,
    development or transformation of;

spiritualizaton): 3, 16, 17, 27, 35, 65, *71–75*, 77–83, 103
institutionalism: 2, 5, 95; in *Il Bidone*, 58, 61; and Catholicism, 14, 18, 23, 25, 41, 43, 46, 47, 48, 70, 75, 115, 116; and language, 17–18; and marriage, 16, 22–23, 31, 33, 41, 48, 70; in "A Matrimonial Agency," 31, 33, 103; in *The Nights of Cabiria*, 70; and Rome, 14–15, 41, 43, 103, 105, 116; in *La Strada*, 41, 42–44, 46, 47–48; in "The Temptations of Dr. Antonio," 115–18; in *I Vitelloni*, 21–24, 25, 26, 27, 28; in *The White Sheik*, 2, 14–18, 110
instrumentalism, 46, 50, 62, 63
linearity (vs. circularity), 37, 38, 105–06
love: 4, 38, 115; absence, illusion, or loss of, 16, 31, 122; in *Il Bidone*, 61, 63; in *La Dolce Vita*, 86–95; in "A Matrimonial Agency," 31; in *La Strada*, 37, 40, 46, 47, 48, 52; in "The Temptations of Dr. Antonio," 115–18; in *I Vitelloni*, 22–23, 24, 25, 26; and spiritual development, 16, 72, 73, 74–75, 76, 77–82
marriage: and the absence of love, 13, 16, 23, 27, 31–34, 93; and dependency, 16, 23, 48, 70; and illusion, 13, 16, 48, 70, 104, 105; and individuation, 16, 78–79, 81, 104; and institutionalism, 16, 22–23, 31, 33, 41, 48, 70
mediation, 24, 25, 31, 37, 56, 58, 60–61, 82, 90, 99
negation (*see also* annulment): 101–02; in *Il Bidone*, 55, 63, 65–66; in *La Dolce Vita*, 66, 87, 90, 91, 93–96, 98, 99; in *I Vitelloni*, 14, 25–26, 108
possibility (vs. givenness): 73, 78, 87, 91, 103–04, 108, 109
projection, psychological and filmic: in *Il Bidone*, 61; in *La Dolce Vita*, 87, 94; in *The Nights of Cabiria*, 72, 73; in *La Strada*, 41–45, 50, 60, 102; in "The Temptations of Dr. Antonio," 115, 116, 119, 120, 122, 124; in *Variety Lights*, 9, 10; in *The White Sheik*, 13

prostitution: 40, 69; in *Il Bidone*, 60–61; in "A Matrimonial Agency," 31; in *The Nights of Cabiria*, 69, 70, 74, 75, 78, 79, 82, 102
provinces, the: 7, 35, 78, 112; and dependency, 15, 17, 21, 26
regression: 5; in *La Dolce Vita*, 87, 90–95, 98; in *La Strada*, 46, 49–50, 51, 52–53, 94; in "The Temptations of Dr. Antonio," 116–18, 122
religious patterns and symbolism: 42–43, 70–71, 73–75, 78–79, 85–86, 87–88, 89, 90, 93, 94–95, 99, 107, 115–18; baptism, 52, 60, 71, 88, 93; Christ imagery, 26, 43, 85, 86–87, 92, 94–95; divinity, 13, 14, 18, 28, 42, 43, 46, 48, 50, 70, 74, 82, 99, 115–18, 122; martyrdom, 26, 43, 47, 48, 63, 65; rebirth, 50, 52, 57, 63, 70, 71, 72, 73, 74, 77, 80, 81, 82, 83, 88, 94–95, 96, 104–05, 107, 117; the Second Coming, 85, 86–87, 88, 89, 99
renewal, authentic: 65–66, 69, 70, 85, 96, 98, 99, 104–05
renewal, inauthentic: 37–38, 55–63, 65–66, 70, 86–95, 104–05
Rome, and illusion, 8, 13, 14–15, 43; and institutionalism, 14–15, 41, 43, 103, 105, 116
rootlessness, 8, 27, 35, 57, 58, 61, 103
self-deception: 10, 13, 32, 34, 61, 65, 102
spectacle. *See* art and artifice
spiral imagery (vs. linearity and circularity), 105–06
spirituality, failed or false, 24, 42, 46, 47–48, 56–57, 63, 64, 70, 85–96, 115–18
spiritualization (*see also* consciousness, development or transformation of; creative experience, imagination, individuation), 3, 5, *70–75*, 77–82, 95–96, 99, 106–07
vision (images), and individuation, 17, 72–73, 82, 111–12

WORKS:
Amarcord, 15, 110; *Il Bidone*, 35, 55–66, 69, 82–83, 93, 94, 95, 96, 102,

103, 104, 105, 106, 107, 108, 110, 112, 122; *City of Women*, 4, 10, 113; *The Clowns*, 4, 108, 113, 124; *La Dolce Vita*, 2, 4, 15, 35, 66, 85–99, 101, 112–13, 115, 117, 118, 122, 123, 124; *8½*, 3, 4, 10, 18, 53, 65, 95, 101, 109, 110, 112, 113, 115, 123, 124, 125; *Fellini: A Director's Notebook*, 5, 108, 113, 124; *Fellini-Satyricon*, 4, 108, 123, 124, 125; *Fellini's Casanova*, 123; *Fellini's Roma*, 4, 15, 65, 101, 108, 113, 124; *Juliet of the Spirits*, 10, 16, 53, 108, 115, 123, 124, 125; "A Matrimonial Agency," 2, 16, *31–35*, 43, 96, 102, 103, 105, 107, 112; "Moraldo in the City" (unrealized project), 35, 85, 87; *The Nights of Cabiria*, 3, 4, 10, 16, 18, 53, 65, 69–83, 85, 87–88, 90, 95, 96, 97, 101, 102–03, 104, 106–07, 108, 109, 110, 111, 112, 113, 118; *La Strada*, 4, 16, 35, *37–53*, 55, 56, 59, 60, 62, 69–70, 82–83, 85, 89–90, 92, 93, 94, 95, 96, 102, 103–04, 105, 107, 108, 109, 110, 112, 122; "The Temptations of Dr. Antonio," 9, 18, 109, *115–25*; "Toby Dammit," 108; *Variety Lights*, *7–10*, 13, 14, 18, 21, 26, 34, 43, 82, 96, 101, 103, 105, 107, 108, 112, 123; *I Vitelloni*, 14, 16, *21–28*, 31, 55, 85, 87, 101, 103, 104, 105, 107, 108, 110, 112; *The White Sheik*, 1, 10, *13–18*, 21, 23, 26, 34, 43, 61, 69, 70, 82, 101, 103, 105, 107, 108, 109, 110, 112, 123

Forster, E.M., 107
Fumetti, 13, 14, 16–17, 18, 110

Garden of the Finzi-Contini, The, 3

Hemingway, Ernest, 2
Hitler, Adolf, 2

King Kong (original version), 120

Lattuada, Alberto, 3, 7, 31
Lilith, 9
Love in the City (Amore in Città), 31

McLuhan, Marshall, 125
Masina, Giulietta (wife of Fellini), 1, 18, 53, 69, 83
Miracle, The, 1
Monicelli, Mario, 115
Mussolini, Benito, 2, 24

Neorealism, 1–5, 31, 34

Oedipus Rex, 107

Paisan, 1
Paterson (William Carlos Williams), 1
Paul, St., 95
Ponti, Carlo, 115

Risi, Dino, 31
Rome, 4, 7, 8, 13, 14–15, 21, 27, 35, 41, 43, 69, 87, 91, 103, 105, 109, 115, 116, 120
Rossellini, Roberto, 1

Sun Also Rises, The, 2–3

Visconti, Luchino, 1, 3, 115

"White Telephone" films, 2
Williams, William Carlos, 1

Zavattini, Cesare, 1, 2, 3, 4, 31